ROBERTO GUERRERO

PPG Salutes 1992 Pole Winner Roberto Guerrero

*W*hen Roberto Guerrero sped around the Indianapolis Motor Speedway to win the $100,000 PPG Pole Award, he instantly became the world's fastest race driver. No driver has ever equaled his 232.482 mph four-lap record on any race track, nor his fastest lap speed of 232.618 mph.

Indy car racing, more than any other sport in the world, requires exceptional skills, intelligence, courage, versatility, concentration and split-second reaction, particularly at such amazing speeds.

Roberto possesses all of these qualities – and more. He has established a new standard of excellence for race drivers around the world, as well as for the people who design, engineer and build the cars we drive on the streets and highways.

The same standard, indeed, that has made PPG automotive finishes the first choice of automotive manufacturers worldwide. Another reason why PPG coatings are found on two of every three cars and trucks made in the free world. And, since 1978, exclusively on all cars competing in the Indianapolis 500.

**PPG
POLE AWARD
INDIANAPOLIS 500**

Designed by PPG designers and crafted by Tiffany's of New York, the PPG Pole Award is fabricated from sterling silver, silicon bronze, fluorescent polymers and crystal glass in unique combinations that exhibit high quality craftsmanship and design. The scoring pylon at the Indianapolis Motor Speedway influenced the dominant vertical statement of the trophy.

Roberto Guerrero receives $100,000 check and trophy from Jim Chapman, PPG's Director of Racing, for the PPG Pole Award. In addition to the pole award, PPG gave a total of $330,000 in prize money, or $10,000 for each of the 33 starting cars, as well as gold rings with green stones, to each of the participants in the 1992 Indianapolis 500.

The Indianapolis 500 is the premier event in the PPG Indy Car World Series, proudly sponsored by PPG Industries since 1980.

CONTENTS

Thank You..4
Mark English - Cover Artist 9
Entry List...11
Trackside Files 19
"500" Festival..52
The 33 Starters 56
For Those Who Tried 102
Before the Roar 107
Race to the Bricks 110
Great Year for Goodyear..............................138
After the Roar 149
Qualifying Awards 153

Special Incentive Awards 154
Contingency Awards 156
USAC and Officials 157
Daily Practice Laps 158
Daily Best Speeds 160
Qualification Attempt Summary.................162
Starting Lineup 163
Interval Scoring...164
Official Box Score...165
Indy's Career Top 10 166
Advertiser's Index/Credits 167

Published by: Indy 500 Publications - IMS Corporation
Executive Editor: William R. Donaldson
Editor: Kurt D. Hunt
Assistant Editor: Dawn M. Bair

Advertising Sales: Kevin A. Davey
Graphic Design: Frederick Jungclaus & Michael Kreffel
Editorial Contributions: Bob Laycock, Jan Shaffer, Lee Driggers,
Gordon Kirby and Donald Davidson.

©Indianapolis Motor Speedway Corporation 1992. All Rights Reserved.
INDY 500 PUBLICATIONS - INDY REVIEW VOLUME 2, 1992   ISBN 1-880526-01-8   Library of Congress ISSN 1059-3179

Rick Mears' 1991 Indy 500-winning Penske 91 Chevrolet.   Exclusive tires: Goodyear Eagle racing radials.

The 1993 Cadillac Allanté Indy 500 Pace Car.   Exclusive tires: Goodyear Eagle GA radials.

Here are two Indy 500 predictions that are bound to come true.

One. More than a quarter of a million people will fill the stands at this year's 76th running of the Indianapolis 500.

Two. The race will be won on Goodyear Eagle racing radials.

How can we be sure? Easy. Every single car in the race will be riding on Goodyear Eagle racing radials.

A "Goodyear Eagle" contact patch. Where an Eagle's superiority is clearly visible.

And naturally, this is not a coincidence.

Race teams and drivers have a sharp eye out for anything that will give them a competitive edge. And Goodyear has long since proved it delivers on the track. Goodyear started its string of victories at the Indianapolis 500 twenty-one races ago. And we've never stopped.

ONCE AGAIN, EVERY CAR AT INDY WILL BE ON ONE MAKE OF TIRE. PREDICTABLY, IT'S GOODYEAR EAGLES.

Like Indy race teams, car manufacturers have a vital interest in tire technology. They look to competitive testing to tell which tires will give their new models the best performance.

The result: more top-of-the-line performance cars come equipped with Goodyear Eagle street radials than any other tire.

Including this year's Indy 500 Pace Car, the 1993 Cadillac Allanté.

Be sure to visit your local Goodyear retailer. Where you'll discover all the advantages of the complete Goodyear Eagle line.

Another prediction that's bound to come true.

THE BEST TIRES IN THE WORLD
HAVE GOODYEAR WRITTEN ALL OVER THEM.

TONY HULMAN, JR.
1901 - 1977

MARY HULMAN

MARI GEORGE

TONY GEORGE

THANK YOU

One year ago we presented the first <u>Indy Review</u> to capture the memories and highlights of the historic 75th running of the "500." We are pleased now to present this publication as the official annual record of "The Greatest Spectacle In Racing."

Every year, history is made at the Indianapolis Motor Speedway. In 1992, Al Unser Jr. became the Speedway's first second-generation champion, following in the footsteps of his father, four-time "500" winner Al Unser. It was a moment my own family treasured in celebration of both tradition and friendship.

Along with Al Jr., we congratulate all members of the winning Galles-Kraco Racing team, which endured a difficult month and a long race en route to Victory Lane. Our congratulations go as well to Scott Goodyear for placing second in the closest Indianapolis 500 finish ever.

It was also a year of unparalleled speed as the 230-mile per hour barrier was eclipsed in qualifying, providing the "500" its fastest 33-car starting field.

To our fans, the entire Hulman-George family appreciates your loyalty through what was an unusually chilly and in many cases uncomfortable race day. It is that loyalty which provides us the opportunity to present to the world every year its richest and most prestigious auto racing event.

Anton H. George
President
Indianapolis Motor Speedway

Every 1993 Cadillac Allanté is built to

OFFICIAL PACE CAR

Every 1993 Cadillac Allanté is technologically identical to the Allanté that will pace this year's Indianapolis 500. Only United States Auto Club racing safety equipment has been added.

This new Allanté marks the first light of the Northstar System, including the all-new 295-horsepower, 4.6L 32-valve Northstar V8 complementing the sophisticated new Road-Sensing Suspension that adjusts instantaneously to optimize driver control.

The 1993 Cadillac Allanté. It could change the way you think about American engineering.

keep pace with some very fast company.

TH INDIANAPOLIS 500

INDIANAPOLIS
THE SEVENTY SIXTH • MAY 24, 1992

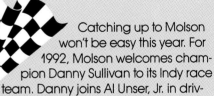

ABOUT THE ARTIST

Mark English is recognized as one of the leading magazine illustrators in the United States. His unique style has been enjoyed by millions on the covers of national publications such as *McCalls, Time, Sports Illustrated, Red Book,* and *Atlantic Monthly.*

Mark has won literally hundreds of awards for his work and holds the distinction of being the most awarded illustrator in the history of the Society of Illustrators in New York.

In 1969, Mark was chosen "Artist of the Year" by the New York Artist Guild and in 1981, he was named one of the top three illustrators in America by *ADVERTISING AGE.*

He has produced nine stamps for the U.S. Postal Service and his work has been exhibited throughout the world in such places as the Nelson Gallery in Kansas City, the Smithsonian Institute and the Brandy Wine Museum.

In 1983, Mark English was elected to "The Illustrators Hall of Fame" in New York joining such notable illustrators as N.C. Wyeth, Maxfield Parrish and Frederick Remington, Robert Peak and Bernie Fuchs.

Mark English has captured on canvas one of the Speedway's most exciting moments, the finish of the 1992 Indy 500. This painting was commissioned for the Miller Wall of Fame located in the Indianapolis Motor Speedway Hall of Fame Museum.

TYPHOON

On September 14, 1990, a modified GMC Truck set a new F.I.A. authenticated record of 204.145 miles per hour, two-way average, in the flying mile. Yes, you read that right. A GMC *Truck*. The street-legal truck inspired by these explorations was a

IF YOU HAVE SETTLED IDEAS OF LUXURY, SAFETY AND PERFORMANCE, A TYPHOON WILL BLOW THEM AWAY.

compact pickup called Syclone. Performance cognoscenti still speak of how *Car and Driver* pitted Syclone against a $122,000 Ferrari 348ts. "In a blink, the Ferrari is looking at tailgate," they wrote.

Now we've taken this experience in power, handling and braking to a new, astonishing level. In Typhoon. The sports coupe of sport utilities.

Brace yourself: Typhoon is riding on the kind of technology you wouldn't expect in a utility vehicle: the same safety and performance technology as Syclone. A 4.3L V6, turbocharged and liquid-intercooled, that yields 280 horse-power. A 4-speed automatic transmission with over-drive top gear. All-wheel drive. And 4-wheel anti-lock braking.

AVAILABLE DELCO CD. LEATHER-TRIMMED SEATING. THE SOUND AND FEEL OF LUXURY.

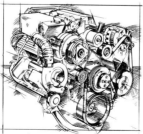

4.3L V6. TURBOCHARGED. A PRACTICAL APPROACH TO SHEER EXUBERANCE.

Typhoon's luxury appointments will be comforts to you, too. Body styling that's easy on the eyes. A leather-trimmed seating area with front bucket seats. Adjustable lumbar supports and side bolsters in the buckets. A Delco AM/FM stereo system with available compact disc player.

Did we mention 67.3 cubic feet of luggage space (with the rear seat folded down)? Typhoon is still, after all, a utility vehicle.

Only from a company with over 80 years of truck experience could a vehicle so wholly unexpected seem so wholly fitting. Call 1-800-879-4621 to find out how to put yourself in the eye of the storm: Typhoon, from GMC Truck.

GMC TRUCK

THE STRENGTH OF EXPERIENCE

GMC, GMC Truck and Typhoon are
registered trademarks of General Motors Corp.

© 1992 GM Corp. All Rights Reserved.
Buckle up, America!

Quality Network

ENTRY LIST

CAR	DRIVER	CAR NAME	YEAR/CHASSIS/ENGINE	ENTRANT
1	Michael Andretti	Kmart/Texaco Newman/Haas Lola	92 Lola / Ford Cosworth XB	Newman/Haas Racing
1 T	Michael Andretti	Kmart/Texaco Newman/Haas Lola	92 Lola / Ford Cosworth XB	Newman/Haas Racing
2	Mario Andretti	Kmart/Texaco Newman/Haas Lola	92 Lola / Ford Cosworth XB	Newman/Haas Racing
2 T	Mario Andretti	Kmart/Texaco Newman/Haas Lola	92 Lola / Ford Cosworth XB	Newman/Haas Racing
3	Al Unser Jr.	Valvoline Galmer '92 Chevrolet	92 Galmer / Chevrolet Indy V8 / A	Galles-Kraco Racing
3 T	Al Unser Jr.	Valvoline Galmer '92 Chevrolet	92 Galmer / Chevrolet Indy V8 /A	Galles-Kraco Racing
4	Rick Mears	Marlboro Penske Chevy 92	92 Penske / Chevrolet Indy V8 / B	Penske Racing, Inc.
4 T	Rick Mears	Marlboro Penske Chevy 92	92 Penske / Chevrolet Indy V8 / B	Penske Racing, Inc.
5	Emerson Fittipaldi	Marlboro Penske Chevy 92	92 Penske /Chevrolet Indy V8 / B	Penske Racing, Inc
5 T	Emerson Fittipaldi	Marlboro Penske Chevy 92	92 Penske / Chevrolet Indy V8 / B	Penske Racing, Inc.
6	Arie Luyendyk	Target/Scotch Video Lola	92 Lola / Ford Cosworth XB	Chip Ganassi Racing Teams, Inc.
6 T	Arie Luyendyk	Target/Scotch Video Lola	91 Lola / Ford Cosworth XB	Chip Ganassi Racing Teams, Inc.
7	Paul Tracy	Mobil 1 Penske Chevy 91	91 Penske / Chevrolet Indy V8 / A	Penske Racing, Inc.
7 T	Paul Tracy	Mobil 1 Penske Chevy 91	91 Penske / Chevrolet Indy V8 / A	Penske Racing, Inc.
8	John Andretti	Pennzoil Special	92 Lola / Chevrolet Indy V8 / A	Hall/VDS Racing, Inc.
8 T	John Andretti	Pennzoil Special	92 Lola / Chevrolet Indy V8/A	Hall/VDS Racing, Inc.
9	Eddie Cheever	Target/Scotch Video Lola	92 Lola / Ford Cosworth XB	Chip Ganassi Racing Teams, Inc.
9 T	Eddie Cheever	Target/Scotch Video Lola	92 Lola / Ford Cosworth XB	Chip Ganassi Racing Teams, Inc.
10	Scott Pruett	Budweiser Eagle Truesports 92C	92 Truesports 92C / Chevrolet Indy V8 / A	Truesports Company
10 T	Scott Pruett	Budweiser Eagle Truesports 92C	92 Truesports 92C / Chevrolet Indy V8 / A	Truesports Company
11 (a)	Hiro Matsushita	Panasonic/SEGA Lola	92 Lola / Chevrolet Indy V8 / A	Dick Simon Racing, Inc.
11 T	Hiro Matsushita	Panasonic/SEGA Lola	92 Lola / Chevrolet Indy V8 / A	Dick Simon Racing, Inc.
12	Bobby Rahal	Miller Genuine Draft Special	92 Lola / Chevrolet Indy V8 / A	Rahal/Hogan Racing, Inc.
12 T	Bobby Rahal	Miller Genuine Draft Special	92 Lola/Chevrolet Indy V8 / A	Rahal/Hogan Racing, Inc.
14	A.J. Foyt, Jr.	A.J. Foyt/Copenhagen Racing	92 Lola / Chevrolet Indy V8 / A	A.J. Foyt Enterprises
15 (b)	Scott Goodyear	Mackenzie Financial Special	92 Lola / Chevrolet Indy V8 / A	Walker Motorsports, Inc.
15 T	Scott Goodyear	Mackenzie Financial Special	91 Lola / Chevrolet Indy V8 / A	Walker Motorsports, Inc.
16	Tony Bettenhausen	AMAX Energy+Metals PC20	91 Penske PC20 / Chevrolet Indy V8 / A	Bettenhausen Motorsports, Inc.
16 T	Tony Bettenhausen	AMAX Energy+Metals PC20	91 Penske PC20 / Chevrolet Indy V8 / A	Bettenhausen Motorsports, Inc.
17	Johnny Rutherford		91 Lola / Chevrolet Indy V8 / A	Walker Motorsports, Inc.
18	Danny Sullivan	Molson/Kraco/STP Galmer '92 Chevrolet	92 Galmer / Chevrolet Indy V8 / A	Galles-Kraco Racing
18 T	Danny Sullivan	Molson/Kraco/STP Galmer '92 Chevrolet	92 Galmer / Chevrolet Indy V8 / A	Galles-Kraco Racing

Nineteen Ninety Won.

Won
Bosch, 4th straight CART/PPG Indy Car championship.

Won
Emerson Fittipaldi, Detroit Grand Prix.

Won
Raul Boesel, IMSA GTP race, Miami.

Won
Roger Mears, SCORE/HDRA Class 7 title.

Won
Rick Mears, The pole at Indy.

Won
Bobby Rahal, Marlboro Grand Prix, Meadowlands.

Won
Bosch, 16th straight IMSA GTP 24-hours at Daytona.

Won
Joe Varde, Firestone Firehawk Grand Sports.

Won
A. J. Foyt, 2nd fastest qualifier, Indy.

Won
Roger Mears, Baja 500, Baja 1000 desert races.

Won
Bosch, 5th straight Indy 500.

Won
Jim Vasser, 6 1st place finishes, Toyota Atlantic series.

Won
Rick Mears, His 4th Indy 500.

Won
Jovy Marcelo, Toyota Atlantic Championship.

Won
Arie Luyendyk, Bosch Spark Plug Grand Prix, Nazareth.

Won
Bosch, 21st straight IMSA GTP Crown.

Won
Geoff Brabham, 4th straight IMSA Camel GTP title.

Won
P. J. Jones, Indy Lights races, Toronto and Denver.

Won
Davy Jones, 5 IMSA GTP victories.

Won
Bob Leitzinger, IMSA GTU race, Del Mar.

Won
Jeff Andretti, CART/PPG Rookie of the Year.

Won
Al Unser, Jr., 4th straight Toyota Grand Prix, Long Beach.

Won
Paul Hacker, 4th Firehawk Sports Class Championship.

Won
John Andretti, the 1st Indy Car race in Australia.

Won
Hurley Haywood, Potenza Supercar Championship.

Won
Robbie Groff, Indy Lights races, Phoenix and Milwaukee.

Won
Eric Bachelart, Firestone Indy Lights Championship.

Won
Bill Elliott, Pepsi 400, Daytona.

Won
Juan Fangio II, IMSA GTP race, Del Mar.

Won
Ivan Stewart, 3 overall and class races in desert racing.

Won
Michael Andretti, 8 poles and 8 Indy Car victories.

Won
Bosch, every Indy Car race in 1991.

Won
Michael Andretti, PPG Cup Indy Car World Series championship.

Won
Steve Millen, 4 IMSA GTO 1st place finishes.

Won
Hurley Haywood, His 5th 24-hours at Daytona.

Won
John Fergus, 1st IMSA GTU Championship.

Won
Jeremy Dale, 2 IMSA GTO division races.

Bosch racers had their winningest year ever. You can get the same kind of winning performance with Bosch Platinum Spark Plugs.

They'll give you quicker starts, smoother acceleration, and improved fuel efficiency. Call 1-800-882-8101 for a Bosch retailer near you.

BOSCH

CAR	DRIVER	CAR NAME	YEAR/CHASSIS/ENGINE	ENTRANT
19	Eric Bachelart	Royal Oak Charcoal/Mi-Jack	90 Lola / Buick V-6	Dale Coyne Racing
21	Buddy Lazier	Leader Cards Lola	90 Lola / Buick V-6	Leader Cards, Inc.
21T	Buddy Lazier	Leader Cards Lola	90 Lola / Buick V-6	Leader Cards, Inc.
22	Scott Brayton	Amway/Northwest Airlines-Winning Spirit Lola	92 Lola / Buick V-6	Dick Simon Racing, Inc.
22T	Scott Brayton	Amway/Northwest Airlines-Winning Spirit Lola	92 Lola / Chevrolet Indy V8 / A	Dick Simon Racing, Inc.
23	TBA		92 Lola / Buick V-6	Dick Simon Racing, Inc.
26	Jim Crawford	Quaker State Buick Lola/King Motorsports	92 Lola / Buick V-6	Kenny Bernstein's King Motorsports
26T	Jim Crawford	Quaker State Buick Lola/King Motorsports	91 Lola / Buick V-6	Kenny Bernstein's King Motorsports
27	Nelson Piquet	CONSECO Special	92 Lola / Buick V-6	Team Menard, Inc.
27T	Nelson Piquet	CONSECO Special	91 Lola / Buick V-6	Team Menard, Inc.
28	TBA		92 Galmer / Chevrolet Indy V8 / A	Galles-Kraco Racing
29	TBA		92 Lola / Chevrolet Indy V8 / A	Dick Simon Racing, Inc.
30	Fabrizio Barbazza	ALFA-LAVAL	90 Lola / Buick V-6	Arciero Racing Teams
31	Ted Prappas	Say No To Drugs/P.I.G. Racing	91 Lola / Chevrolet Indy V8 / A	Norman C. Turley
31T	Ted Prappas	Say No To Drugs/P.I.G. Racing	91 Lola / Chevrolet Indy V8 / A	Norman C. Turley
33	TBA	A.J. Foyt/Copenhagen Racing	90 Lola / Chevrolet Indy V8 / A	A.J. Foyt Enterprises
34	Jeff Wood	Rent A Center/Pioneer Karaoke Houston Special	91 Lola / Buick V-6	Arciero Racing Teams
35	TBA	Marlboro Penske Chevy 91	91 Penske / Chevrolet Indy V8 / A	Penske Racing, Inc.
36	Roberto Guerrero	Quaker State Buick Lola/King Motorsports	92 Lola / Buick V-6	Kenny Bernstein's King Motorsports
36T	Roberto Guerrero	Quaker State Buick Lola/King Motorsports	91 Lola / Buick V-6	Kenny Bernstein's King Motorsports
38	John Andretti	Pennzoil Special	91 Lola / Chevrolet Indy V8 / A	Hall/VDS Racing, Inc.
39	Brian Bonner	Applebee's/DANKA	91 Lola / Buick V-6	Dale Coyne Racing
41	TBA	A.J. Foyt/Copenhagen Racing	92 Lola / Chevrolet Indy V8 / A	A.J. Foyt Enterprises
42	TBA	Euro International Fendi AGIP IEMA Taumarin Slam	91 Lola / Cosworth DFS	Euromotorsport Racing Inc.
44	Philippe Gache	Formula Project-Rhone Poulenc Rorer	91 Lola / Chevrolet Indy V8 / A	Formula Project/Dick Simon Racing
44T(c)	Philippe Gache	Formula Project-Rhone Poulenc Rorer	91 Lola / Chevrolet Indy V8 / A	Formula Project/Dick Simon Racing
47	Jimmy Vasser	Kodalux/Hayhoe-Cole Special	91 Lola / Chevrolet Indy V8 / A	Hayhoe-Cole Racing, Inc.
47T	Jimmy Vasser	Kodalux/Hayhoe-Cole Special	91 Lola / Chevrolet Indy V8 / A	Hayhoe-Cole Racing, Inc.
48	Jeff Andretti	Gillette/Carlo/Texaco	91 Lola / Buick V-6	A.J. Foyt/Copenhagen Racing
50	Jovy Marcelo	Euromotorsport Fendi AGIP Marcelo Midas Taumarin	91 Lola / Cosworth DFS	Euromotorsport Racing, Inc.
50T	Jovy Marcelo	Euromotorsport Fendi AGIP Taumarin IEMA Slam	90 Lola / Cosworth DFS	Euromotorsport Racing, Inc.
51	Gary Bettenhausen	Glidden Paints Special	92 Lola / Buick V-6	Team Menard, Inc.

CAR	DRIVER	CAR NAME	YEAR/CHASSIS/ENGINE	ENTRANT
51T (d)	Gary Bettenhausen	Glidden Paints Special	92 Lola / Buick V-6	Team Menard, Inc.
53	TBA		90 Penske / Chevrolet Indy V8 / A	Penske Racing, Inc.
54	TBA		90 Penske / Chevrolet Indy V8 / A	Penske Racing, Inc.
56	Michael Andretti	Kmart/Texaco Newman/Haas Lola	91 Lola / Ford Cosworth XB	Newman/Haas Racing
59	Tom Sneva	Menard/Glidden/ Conseco Special	91 Lola / Buick V-6	Team Menard, Inc.
61	TBA	Bettenhausen Motorsports, Inc.	90 Penske PC19/ Chevrolet Indy V8 / A	Bettenhausen Motorsports, Inc.
62	Geoff Brabham	Budweiser Eagle Truesports 92C	92 Truesports 92C / Chevrolet Indy V8/A	Truesports Company
65	Mario Andretti	Kmart/Texaco Newman/Haas Lola	92 Lola / Ford Cosworth XB	Newman/Haas Racing
66	Mark Dismore	Comet Kart Sales/Concept Motorsports	90 Lola / Buick V-6	Concept Motorsports, Inc
68	Dominic Dobson	Burns Racing/Tobacco Free America	91 Lola / Chevrolet Indy V8	Burns Racing Team, Inc.
68T	Dominic Dobson	Burns Racing/Tobacco Free America	90 Lola / Buick V-6	Burns Racing Team, Inc.
70	Bobby Rahal	Miller Genuine Draft Special	TBA / Chevrolet Indy V8 / A	Rahal/Hogan Racing Inc.
71	TBA	Jonathan Byrd's Cafeteria/Bryant Heating & Cooling	Lola / Buick V-6	Hemelgarn/Byrd Racing
77	TBA	UNO Racing	91 Lola / TBA	Uno Racing, Inc.
78	TBA	UNO Racing	Lola / TBA	UNO Racing, Inc.
81	TBA	Jonathan Byrd's Cafeteria/Bryant Heating & Cooling	Lola / Buick V-6	Hemelgarn/Byrd Racing
84	TBA	A.J. Foyt/Copenhagen Racing	91 Lola / Chevrolet Indy V8 / A	A.J. Foyt Enterprises
88	Kenji Momota	CAPCOM/TEAMKAR	91 Lola / Chevrolet Indy V8 / A	TEAMKAR International, Inc.
88T	Kenji Momota	CAPCOM/TEAMKAR	90 Lola / Chevy Indy V8 / A	TEAMKAR International, Inc.
90	Lyn St. James	Agency Rent-A-Car/JCPenney "Spirit of the American Woman"	91 Lola / Chevrolet Indy V8	Paragon Motorsports, Inc.
90T	Lyn St. James	Agency Rent-A-Car/JCPenney "Spirit of the American Woman"	91 Lola / Cosworth DFS-90	Paragon Motorsports, Inc.
91	Stan Fox	Jonathan Byrd's Cafeteria/Bryant Heating & Cooling	91 Lola / Buick V-6	Hemelgarn/Byrd Racing
92	Gordon Johncock	STP/Jack's Tool Rental/Hemelgarn	91 Lola / Buick V-6	Hemelgarn/Runyan Racing
93	John Paul, Jr.	D.B. Mann Development Buick	90 Lola / Buick V-6	D.B. Mann Motorsports
93T	John Paul, Jr.	D.B. Mann Development Buick	90 Lola / Buick V-6	D.B. Mann Motorsports
94	TBA	Hemelgarn Racing	Lola / Buick V-6	Hemelgarn Racing, Inc.
95	TBA	UNO Racing	91 Lola / TBA	UNO Racing, Inc.
96	TBA	D.B. Mann Development Buick	Lola / Buick V-6	D.B. Mann Motorsports
97	Steve Chassey	CNC System Sales Baker Machinery Miyano Lola	91 Lola / Buick V-6	R. Kent Baker Racing Inc.
98	TBA	Hemelgarn Racing	Lola / Buick V-6	Hemelgarn Racing, Inc.
99	TBA	Hemelgarn Racing	Lola / Buick V-6	Hemelgarn Racing, Inc.

Entry list as of May 18, 1992. (a) #11 qualified and driven in race by Raul Boesel; (b) #15 qualified by Mike Groff and driven in race by S. Goodyear; (c) #44T qualified by Lyn St. James and raced as #90; (d) #51T qualified and raced as #27 by Al Unser.

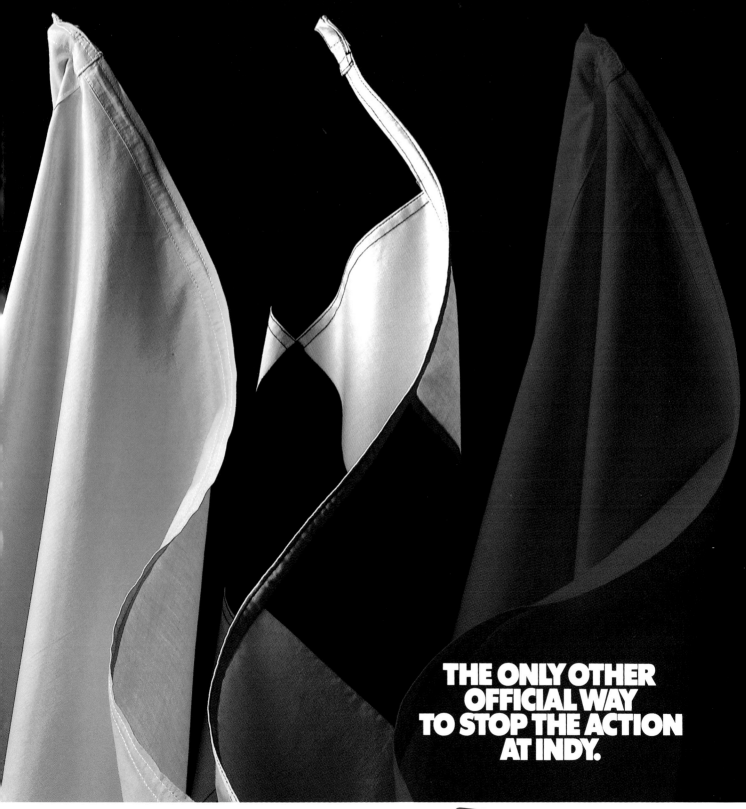

THE ONLY OTHER OFFICIAL WAY TO STOP THE ACTION AT INDY.

KODAK FILM, THE OFFICIAL FILM OF THE INDY 500,

GIVES QUALITY-DRIVEN PHOTOGRAPHERS

THE HIGH PERFORMANCE THEY NEED. AND THEN SOME.

NO WONDER IT'S IN THE POLE POSITION THE WORLD OVER.

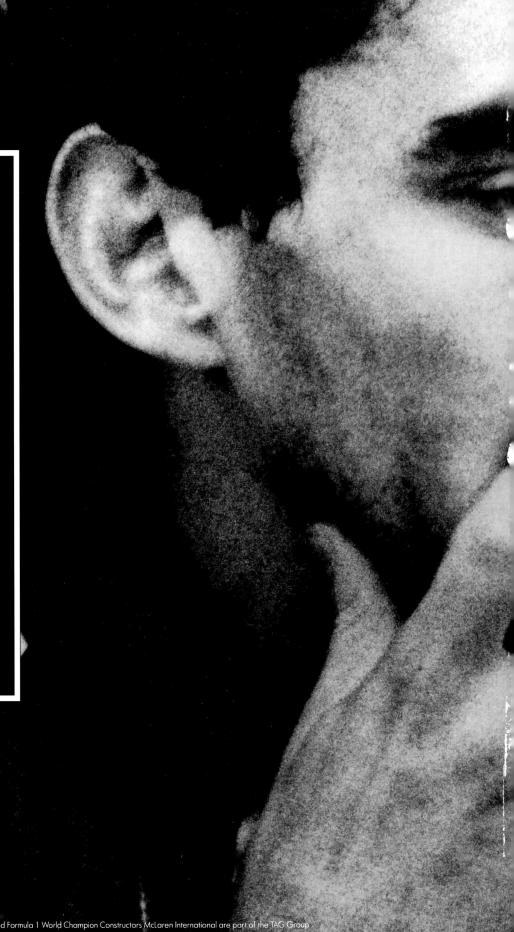

DON'T CRACK UNDER PRESSURE

TAG-Heuer watches possess endurance and precision: qualities found among those who thrive on pressure. The Series 2000 with a double protection screw-in crown is water-resistant to 200 meters (660 feet). It features a unidirectional turning bezel, a scratch-resistant sapphire crystal, and a double safety lock on metal bracelet.

TAG-Heuer
SWISS MADE SINCE 1860

TAG-HEUER. THE OFFICIAL SPORTS WATCH OF THE 1992 INDY 500.®

INDIANAPOLIS
500
THE SEVENTY SIXTH · MAY 24, 1992

The following chronology of the Month of May, 1992, was written by Jan Shaffer, Trackside Report Editor for the Speedway, and edited by IMS Historian Bob Laycock. The information was compiled under the direction of Bob Walters, the Speedway's Director of Public Relations.

Contributing to this chronicle as the month of May unfolded were Speedway Press Room Manager Bill York and staffer Bob Clidinst; the Trackside Report team of assistant Janine Vogrin and staffers Gwynda Eversole, Daryle Feistman, Ruth Ann Cadou Hofmann, Lucy Jackson, Becky Lenhard, Vern Morseman, Suzanne Robinson and Debbie Shaffer; and Speedway Computer Services Manager Lee Driggers and staffers Tony Hofmann and Richard Smith.

Traditionally, opening day at the track in May is a time when drivers and teams are still setting up shop for the long haul.

A few cars take the track for shakedowns, but the race for speed doesn't start until later.

Not so in 1992.

Thirty cars took the track, breaking the modern mark of 24 for a first day in both 1981 and 1988.

And Jim Crawford ran the fastest practice lap in Speedway history at 5:24 p.m., averaging 229.609 miles an hour in the King Motorsports Quaker State Buick.

Crawford's run broke the previous mark of 228.502 set by Al Unser, Jr., on May 11, 1990. He ran only 14 laps.

"The credit's got to go to the team for today," Crawford said. "I wasn't out there long enough to notice anything (about track conditions). I think I did three laps (before the 229-plus)."

"Splits" were available at IMS for the first time through the new USAC/Speedway timing and scoring system, measuring speeds at six points around the course.

Crawford's hot lap showed speeds of 236.2 at the start-finish line, 235.1 near the end of the front straight, 227.0 in turn #2, 232.1 on the backstretch, 233.8 in turn #3 and 225.2 in turn #4.

By 3:30 p.m., Paul Tracy, Jimmy Vasser, Nelson Piquet, Philippe Gache, Kenji Momota and Jovy Marcelo had passed the final phase of their driver's tests. USAC steward Art Meyers said the six were the most to be voted on at once by veteran drivers after observation. Near the end of the day, Lyn St. James became the seventh rookie to be okayed.

Piquet was second fastest of the day in a Team Menard entry at 225.875, followed by Crawford's teammate, Roberto Guerrero, at 225.242.

Opening day is traditionally a day for Dick Simon Racing to capture the attention of the

Top; Disney's Enchanted Castle entry participated in the traditional Balloon Race. Right; Speedway High School Pom Pons performed during opening ceremonies.

amassed by being "first out," and the team did it with a flair not previously seen at the Speedway.

John O. Grettenberger, general manager of Cadillac Motor Division and vice president of General Motors, presented the keys to the candy-apple-red 1993 Cadillac Allanté pace car to IMS President Tony George to signify the opening of the track.

And Simon Racing, which had been "first out" for four straight years, was ready.

The Simon fleet of four cars, to be driven by Scott Brayton, Hiro Matsushita, St. James and Gache were lined up "LeMans style" on pit road, with Matsushita's the closest to the pit exit, followed by Brayton's, St. James' and Gache's.

Simon was going to let his whole team run for the honor.

When the track went green at 1:11 p.m., Michael Fink fired Brayton's car first and Brayton got the jump to the outside of Matsushita. Brayton passed Matsushita on pit road and led into turn #1, followed by Matsushita, St. James and Gache.

The first time past the grandstand, the cars were four abreast in parade fashion, the idea

Date:	Saturday, May 2
Weather:	Overcast, High 79 degrees
Drivers on Track:	25
Cars on Track:	31
Total Laps:	1,015

Top Five Drivers of the Day:		
Car	Driver	Speed
26	Jim Crawford	229.609
27	Nelson Piquet	225.875
36	Roberto Guerrero	225.242
22	Scott Brayton	224.065
51	Gary Bettenhausen	222.574

of Simon's son, Richie. The sight brought cheers from the crowd and tears to Simon's eyes.

"They're all competitive," Simon said. "I told them if they crashed, they weren't the professional drivers I thought they were. Each crew was sitting there talking about how they were going to try to get their car out quicker."

Before the day was over, eight cars had surpassed 220 miles an hour. And it was only Day #1.

Dick Simon's four car stable swept "first out" honors for the fifth straight year.

While Jim Crawford rested on his laurels and sat out the day, others quickly built up to competitive speeds.

Michael Andretti was the fastest of Day #2 with a lap of 226.187 miles an hour in the Kmart/Texaco Newman/Haas Ford Cosworth/Lola, three miles an hour off Crawford's pace.

"The car's good," Andretti said. "The engine seems to be good. Believe it or not, we only ran six or seven hot laps. We don't have it quite right yet but it's comfortable."

The wind was 15 miles an hour out of the northwest, and that played havoc with the team's efforts.

"The wind upsets the balance in turns #1 and #2," Andretti said. "It gives it understeer. You're coming into the turn much quicker because of the tailwind, which makes it push."

But the day wasn't important as much for another hot lap as it was for the number of drivers who got up to speed. The top 10 drivers exceeded 221.5 miles an hour.

Previously, 10 drivers didn't exceed 220 until Day #4 in 1991, Day #7 in 1990 and Day #3 in 1989. In 1988, only two drivers surpassed 220 for the whole month.

The top 10 ranged from Michael Andretti's fastest lap to John Andretti's 221.511 in the Pennzoil Special.

The first accident of the month occurred at 2:30 p.m. when Fabrizio Barbazza, in the #30 ALFA-LAVAL entry went high through turn #1 and hit the wall, slid along it and wound up in turn #2. The car sustained right front damage but Barbazza was uninjured.

Barbazza had just passed his refresher test on the previous lap. Earlier, rookie Eric Bachelart had become the eighth rookie to pass a driver's test.

Off the track, the 12th annual Save Arnold Day for Indiana Special Olympics was held in the Speedway's flag lot and a record 7,000 tickets were sold. Through the years, $1,000,000 has been raised through the program, which was founded by Speedway Chairman Mari Hulman George.

Many drivers take time off from practice to serve as honorary coaches for Special Olympians. For 1992, Al Unser, Lyn St. James, Scott Brayton, Mario Andretti, Tero Palmroth, Jim Crawford, Johnny Rutherford, Tony Bettenhausen, Mike Groff, Jeff Andretti, Philippe Gache and Buddy Lazier led teams in softball activities.

"It's an important thing," Bettenhausen said. "It's fun to root them on and be an influence."

"It's great to come out here with these guys," said Groff.

After that, it was back to the Speedway.

	Date:	Sunday, May 3
	Weather:	Sunny, High 66 degrees
	Drivers on Track:	30
	Cars on Track:	37
	Total Laps:	1,555

Top Five Drivers of the Day:

Car	Driver	Speed
1	Michael Andretti	226.187
36	Roberto Guerrero	226.034
27	Nelson Piquet	225.677
2	Mario Andretti	224.713
5	Emerson Fittipaldi	224.159

Top; Indiana Special Olympians enjoyed their annual day at the track. Left; Mario Andretti exercised his new Ford Lola, checking in as fourth fastest of the day.

Speeds reached new alltime milestones on this day. If you were going to fight for the top of the heap, for the first time in IMS history, you had to exceed 230 miles an hour.

Three drivers did.

The turbocharged stock-block Buick Indy V6, the only production-based engine in the sport, showed its promise in the hands of Roberto Guerrero and Jim Crawford. Cool temperatures, with a high of 59 degrees, helped.

Guerrero, in a King Motorsports Quaker State Buick, became the first driver in Speedway history to exceed 230 miles an hour when he hit 230.432 miles an hour at 11:44 a.m.

Three hours later, Crawford reeled off a lap of 232.198, the first lap ever at IMS in the 38-second bracket. His start-finish line speed was 240.

At 4:47 p.m., Michael Andretti became the third driver to eclipse the 230-mile-an-hour barrier with a lap at 230.852.

Marlboro public relations staffer Kevin Diamond chauffers Emerson Fittipaldi, Nelson Piquet and Paul Tracy.

Crawford upped the ante at 5:53 p.m. with a lap of 233.433 to become fastest of the day. He hit 238 on both straightaways and more than 230 in all four corners.

For Guerrero and Crawford, the unprecedented runs seemed to come relatively easy, although Crawford was surprised by his speeds. The engine in Guerrero's car was its original powerplant and had 420 miles on it.

"It's no surprise to me," Guerrero said. "It's a beautiful day, similar to conditions we ran in testing (in March). I got a 'tow' from (Scott) Pruett when I was still warming up at 226, but the others, I was on my own.

"The chassis is working like a dream. It's producing more downforce than last year, so you can trim it out more for the straightaways and get the same amount of downforce. With good weather, there's definitely more left. No question about it."

Crawford said his car worked like a dream.

"I was surprised," he said about his 233-plus

	Date:	Monday, May 4
	Weather:	Mostly Cloudy, High 59
	Drivers on Track:	31
	Cars on Track:	35
	Total Laps:	1,454

Top Five Drivers of the Day:

Car	Driver	Speed
26	Jim Crawford	233.433
1	Michael Andretti	230.852
36	Roberto Guerrero	230.432
2	Mario Andretti	229.504
51	Gary Bettenhausen	228.490

lap. "I was working toward making the car comfortable. It was so good. It did everything you wanted."

About his earlier, 232-plus effort, Crawford questioned whether he got a "tow."

"I got a little bit of help from Scott Brayton," he said. "He must've been going pretty quick because I didn't pick up that much on him. He crossed the finish line about 75 yards ahead of me. It may not have helped that much, but people will say it did."

Three hours later, he ran faster, anyway.

While Guerrero, Crawford and Michael Andretti chalked up big numbers, others were also finding speed. Ten drivers traveled more than 224.517 miles an hour, the fastest top 10 practice speeds of any day in Speedway history. The previous mark was 10 drivers at more than 224.009 on Day #5 of 1991 (May 6).

Nelson Piquet's fastest lap of the day at 226.809 miles an hour in a Team Menard machine was the fastest ever recorded by a rookie at IMS.

Others found speed quickly. Stan Fox, who had taken 11 laps on Sunday, took nine practice laps today. The car, the Jonathan Byrd's Cafeteria/Bryant Heating and Cooling entry, was the last 1991 Lola specifically built to house the Buick engine.

Fox reached 223.231 miles an hour on the 20th lap the car had ever run. Eight laps later, he reached 225.762.

In the conference room, three-time "500" winner Johnny Rutherford was announced to drive an entry for Walker Motorsports in a bid for a 25th career start.

The deal reunited Rutherford with Derrick Walker, who were matched together on the Penske team in 1984 after Rick Mears was injured at Sanair Super Speedway in Quebec.

But the numbers to reach the front of the lineup were going up.

The boxcar speeds of Day #3 caused the masterminds of several teams to scratch their heads in thought about ways to overhaul the front-running Buicks of Jim Crawford and Roberto Guerrero.

The cooler temperatures, with a high of 57 on Day #4, helped some teams.

But Guerrero was still fastest of the day at 230.149 miles an hour at 2:22 p.m.

Dick Simon Racing was one of the teams enmeshed in thought. It had intended to use its Chevy Indy V/8A-powered machine for Scott Brayton, but it was the sole Chevy team on hand with a Buick backup "in the barn."

With Crawford and Guerrero at comfortably more than 230 miles an hour, Simon had thoughts of going to the Buick.

"If we have a shot for the pole, we'll probably run the Buick," Simon said at 2:30 p.m. "If we don't, we'll unquestionably run the Chevy. Probably on Thursday night, we'll make some sort of decision and concentrate on that car all day Friday."

However, a major element of that decision was changed just a half-hour later. Brayton's Buick-powered mount was smoking going into turn #3, did a three-quarter spin out of turn #4 and slammed the wall with the left side. Brayton suffered only slight bruises to his feet and was cleared to drive, but the car sustained heavy left side and front-end damage.

"It looks like we made our decision," Brayton said.

After Simon got a look at the damage, he said the car was repairable, but not for pole qualifying just four days away.

Others also had problems.

Paul Tracy, in the Mobil 1 Penske Chevy, came out of the pits and got sideways in the middle of turn #1, sliding up to the wall and heavily damaging the right side and nose. Tracy suffered a bruised right arm and left knee.

Buddy Lazier narrowly avoided disaster when he did a complete spin in the Leader Card machine in turn #1, narrowly missing both Hiro Matsushita's car, which was coming on to the track, and the wall.

"As I was leaving pit row, I noticed a wild, spinning object coming at me in my mirrors," Matsushita said. "I'm sure he came within three or four feet of me."

Lyn St. James was also having problems in her bid to become the second woman ever to start the "500." She reached 217.097 miles an

	Date:	Tuesday, May 5
	Weather:	Overcast, High 57 degrees
	Drivers on Track:	28
	Cars on Track:	31
	Total Laps:	1,172

Top Five Drivers of the Day:

Car	Driver	Speed
36	Roberto Guerrero	230.149
2	Mario Andretti	229.990
1	Michael Andretti	229.879
51	Gary Bettenhausen	228.588
6	Arie Luyendyk	228.079

hour, her fastest of the month, but well off the pace.

"The car was flat all the way around and I couldn't go any faster," she said. "Luckily I did because we had an oil leak. This morning, the transducer in the computer went out."

On the brighter side, rookie Ted Prappas passed his refresher in the Say No to Drugs/P.I.G. Racing entry. His car was fitted with a unique head rest to help Prappas keep his head and neck steady.

Rookie Paul Tracy trashed a Penske backup car in turn one.

"Our chief mechanic, John Weland, had seen something similar," Prappas said. "It's made of two-part foam, like the seat, and covers the back and right rear of the cockpit. Apparently it works. I've had no problem with lift or buffeting."

The top 10 of the day ranged from Guerrero's hot lap to Rick Mears' 225.932. In 1991, the top practice speed of the month was by Emerson Fittipaldi on Day #7 (May 10) at 226.705. By mid-afternoon on this day, the top eight drivers had put 1991's best in their pockets.

King Motorsports drivers Roberto Guerrero and Jim Crawford continued to show the rest of the "500" entry list the short way around on this day, which fueled promise for some and a frightening setback for Rick Mears.

The juggle at the top started when Guerrero hit 230 miles an hour for the third day in a row with a lap of 231.558 at 2:49 p.m.

Then Mario Andretti became the month's fourth driver to exceed 230 with a lap of 230.994 at 4:18 p.m. His teammate and son, Michael, hit 230 for the second straight day with a circuit of 231.535 at 5:02 p.m.

Crawford, though, set them all on their heels with a 233.239 mile-an-hour lap at 5:39 p.m. The Flying Scotsman was three miles an hour faster in turns #2 and #4 on his fastest lap than on three previous 231-mile-an-hour laps.

"It was completely different," Crawford said. "The winds were different and I was out there trying to make adjustments. The Andrettis are going fast. They have something up their sleeve."

While King Motorsports and Newman/Haas were in the speed parade, Mears was fortunate to escape serious injury in a horrifying crash in the second turn.

Mears was shaking down his backup machine, last year's mount which was the "500" winner, at 4:26 p.m. when a broken water pipe spewed water under the tires.

In the middle of turn #2, the car did a three-quarter spin to the outside wall, became airborne, came down on the left side and pinwheeled for 730 feet. Mears suffered a minor fracture to his left foot and sprained his right wrist, but was released from Methodist Hospital in good condition.

The car sustained heavy nose and left-side damage, a further setback for the Penske team.

A little more than an hour later, rookie Kenji Momota lost control off turn #4, smacked the outside wall and came to a stop after tapping the inside wall. Momota was hospitalized for overnight observation at Methodist and the car needed right-side repairs.

While those cars went back

Top; Belgian Didier Theys stepped into the Hall/VDS backup ride. Right; Four-time winner Rick Mears took a wild ride through turn two when a water pipe broke in his engine.

	Date:	Wednesday, May 6
	Weather:	Sunny, High 62 degrees
	Drivers on Track:	33
	Cars on Track:	37
	Total Laps:	1,321

Top Five Drivers of the Day:

Car	Driver	Speed
26	Jim Crawford	233.239
36	Roberto Guerrero	231.558
1	Michael Andretti	231.535
2	Mario Andretti	231.124
9	Eddie Cheever	229.550

to the garage, the Simon team had some good news about its Buick-powered car that Scott Brayton had crashed a day earlier.

Chief mechanic Mark Bridges said the car could be repaired as early as Thursday morning, two days earlier than originally figured.

"We had to put another motor in it," Bridges said. "It ripped the tub but didn't damage the bulkhead and suspension points. That's what really saved us. The bottom line is we're unlucky on one hand and lucky on the other."

Didier Theys was named to drive the backup Pennzoil Special for Hall/VDS, adding another car-driver combination to the picture.

But Crawford and Guerrero were still the drivers to beat.

Roberto Guerrero roared into the 230 mile-an-hour bracket for the fourth day in a row and Arie Luyendyk became the fifth driver of the month in the 230-mile-an-hour club as the top seven drivers climbed over 228.

The speed derby was interrupted, however, with a serious accident that sidelined Formula One titlist Nelson Piquet early in his first month of May.

Michael Andretti was the first driver to reach 230 at 2:22 p.m., and later upped his best of the day to 232.012. Guerrero hit his day's best of 232.624 at 4:46 p.m., just before the track's "Happy Hour" shootout.

Luyendyk was next at 5:09 p.m., reaching 230.084. Both Andretti and Luyendyk were powered by Ford engines in its return to Indy, and their efforts didn't go unnoticed. But Guerrero's Buick was still on top.

"The car was actually getting away from me yesterday," Guerrero said. "I was chasing the setup and got it back today. Staying with the track is the trick."

Piquet had also upped his stock in the week-long practice for a shot at the pole position.

Date:	Thursday, May 7
Weather:	Sunny, High 68 degrees
Drivers on Track:	31
Cars on Track:	36
Total Laps:	1,197

Top Five Drivers of the Day:

Car	Driver	Speed
36	Roberto Guerrero	232.624
1	Michael Andretti	232.012
6	Arie Luyendyk	230.084
2	Mario Andretti	229.673
26	Jim Crawford	229.515

Piquet had his best lap of the month, at 228.571, but at 2:35 p.m., just after a yellow light had come on, he hit the outside wall head-on off the fourth turn, suffering multiple fractures of both lower legs and feet.

An examination of the accident by USAC Technical Director Mike Devin revealed that Piquet ran over "a small piece of aluminum" on the backstretch but that the part "doesn't seem to have any bearing on the accident."

"We found a piece that came off another car and that's why the yellow came on," Devin said. "Immediately as the yellow came on, he ran over the part on the back straightaway. Goodyear said the tires were 'flat spotted/inflated,' which means that when he spun, they had air in them."

"It's a very tough situation," said Emerson Fittipaldi, Piquet's close friend from their native Brazil. "Nelson was doing so well at his first Indy. He was very excited to race here. It's just a shame."

Meanwhile, the Penske team shuffled its deck to get another 1992 chassis ready as a backup. It shipped in a car that had been damaged in a testing mishap at Nazareth, Pa., earlier to reconstruct another mount.

But Michael Andretti's close proximity to Guerrero on this day and Luyendyk also at 230 gave the Ford stable some life.

Top; Former World Champion and Indy rookie Nelson Piquet ended his month with an afternoon crash in turn four. **Left;** Roberto Guerrero kept the Buick-powered machines on top of the speed charts.

The Ford assault of Day #6 cast a new look on pole odds, even though Buick drivers still had the upper hand.

But Ford let it be known in earnest that it was a serious contender for the pole on Day #7, leading the way with Mario Andretti's lap of 233.202 miles an hour.

Arie Luyendyk, in another Ford-powered Lola, was next at 232.654, leaving King Motorsports drivers Roberto Guerrero and Jim Crawford with third and fourth of the day in the 231-mile-an-hour bracket.

It was the first day of the month that Mario Andretti had been top gun, with the pole position to be decided the next day.

"There was nobody in front of me on the lap I did 233," Mario said. "The cars (his and Michael's) are very close but they're a little different. On the computer, the way we go through the corner is a little different."

Meanwhile, team owner John Menard named four-time "500" winner Al Unser to replace the injured Nelson Piquet, STP announced sponsorship of the Hemelgarn-Byrd entry to be driven by Gordon Johncock and NASCAR great Richard Petty made his annual visit to the Speedway as part of his Fan Appreciation Tour.

"It's going to be a learning experience," Unser said at the Menard announcement. "It's been two years. It takes awhile to adjust."

Rick Mears and Kenji Momota were cleared to drive by Dr. Henry Bock, the Speedway's

medical director, after their earlier mishaps.

"Yesterday, I felt like a truck ran over me," Mears said. "I couldn't see the wall when I crashed. Before I hit, my first thought was, 'This is going to hurt.'"

The Menard team had a setback for the second straight day, when Gary Bettenhausen, with his backup machine smoking heavily, spun and hit the wall in turn #1. Bettenhausen was uninjured and the machine had only slight right-side damage.

Meanwhile, calls and fax messages came from around the world to inquire and offer words of support for Piquet. A fax and several calls from Fernando Collor, President of Brazil....a call from a friend in South Africa....requests for information from media representatives.

Dr. Bock and Dr. Terry Trammell, who led

Top; Gary Bettenhausen sent a Menard backup car back to the barn after a meeting with the turn one wall. **Right;** Arie Luyendyk consistently appeared as one of the top five drivers of the day during the first week of practice.

the surgical team which operated on Piquet the previous night, held a press conference on the procedures, which had taken 6 1/2 hours.

"There were devastating injuries to his left foot and ankle," said Dr. Trammell. "We were able to reconstruct the left foot and ankle. Circulation to his feet is excellent. He'll go back to surgery Sunday, a 'housecleaning' to make sure there's no debris in the wounds and muscle. It'll take the best part of a year to recover from his injuries. To what degree he recovers, it's too early to tell."

For others, it was on to Pole Day.

Date:	Friday, May 8	
Weather:	Sunny, High 66 degrees	
Drivers on Track:	33	
Cars on Track:	39	
Total Laps:	1,339	

Top Five Drivers of the Day:

Car	Driver	Speed
2	Mario Andretti	233.202
6	Arie Luyendyk	232.654
36	Roberto Guerrero	231.660
26	Jim Crawford	231.344
9	Eddie Cheever	228.443

Top; Car owner John Menard and team captain Gary Bettenhausen chose Al Unser Sr. to replace injured Nelson Piquet. Left; Although Friday was a busy day for qualification-preparation, Bobby Rahal found time to visit with his fans.

DAY 8
SATURDAY, MAY 9

Top; Jim Crawford's morning crash in turn three delayed his attempt for pole position. Bottom; Hiro Matsushita lost his chance for a second Indy start after collecting fluids on the track and crashing in turn one.

When rain hits on the first qualifying day at Indianapolis, the run for the pole can be a cat-and-mouse game of strategy.

Sometimes the pole doesn't go to the swiftest, but the slickest. But in the case of Pole Day, 1992, there was little anyone could do except wait and take your turn. It was the luck of the draw.

The 8 a.m. practice was delayed by rain, and weather and the so-called "weepers," where water came up through the track's surface from below, kept track time slow until 1:35 p.m.

Three minutes later, Jim Crawford spun the Quaker State Buick Lola King Motorsports entry in turn #3 after an apparent engine failure. He didn't make contact with the wall, but it set up a required engine change.

At 2:19 p.m., Hiro Matsushita apparently slid in some fluid from another car in turn #1 and crashed into the outside wall, sending him to Methodist Hospital with a broken right thigh. After "ons and offs," Roberto Guerrero wound up quickest at 232.090.

"I'm ready and I'll be out there as soon as it's my turn," he said.

Michael Andretti wound up second fastest at 231.178 miles an hour. But by then, it was 3:14 p.m., and whether Andretti, who was far back

in the batting order, would get the chance to qualify on this day was chancy at best.

When asked if he could maintain his speed for four consecutive laps, he replied, "Not if I have to run tomorrow. It'll be a lot tougher tomorrow. This is the first real shot I've had at the pole, but it looks like that's the way it's gonna turn out (qualify Sunday)."

Arie Luyendyk was first out at 4 p.m., with two hours of time remaining. He set track records of 229.305 for a single lap and 229.127 for a four-lap average to give the field some big numbers to view.

Rookie Philippe Gache was next with an average of 221.496, becoming the first Frenchman since Rene Dreyfus and Rene Lebegue in 1940 to make a "500" field.

Waveoffs and "safe" qualifiers missed or made the show until Gary Bettenhausen went out at 4:48. He jumped in front of Luyendyk with a track record single lap of 229.317 but his four-lap average was 228.932, good for second spot at the time.

For the 20th qualification attempt of the day, at 5:34 p.m., Roberto Guerrero went out to take his shot. He hooked up four steady laps in the 232 mile-an-hour bracket with a best of 232.618 and an average of 232.482 to take the pole at the time.

"I saw them on the dial and they looked pretty good," Guerrero said of the speeds on his run. "The car was beautiful. From the first time I sat in the car, in March I think, I knew the car was a dream."

After Rick Mears qualified, Mario Andretti put his Ford-powered Lola on the front row at 229.503, joining Guerrero and Luyendyk.

By the end of the day, the one-lap track record had been broken three times and the four-lap average had fallen twice. Eighteen cars had qualified.

Only four cars were left in the original qualifying line with a shot at the pole on Sunday, but two of those four, driven by Eddie Cheever and Michael Andretti, seemed to have the possibility of unseating Guerrero.

Top; Roberto Guerrero set both the one and four-lap track records on his way to capturing the pole position. Left; Roberto's wife Katie anxiously awaited his arrival at the start/finish line.

Others set marks less than Guerrero's strong run. Bobby Rahal, in the Miller Genuine Draft Special, posted the most consistent qualifying run in IMS history with four laps just .006 of a second apart.

Bettenhausen's run broke his own marks for turbocharged stock block engines set a year earlier.

The 18-car field average was 223.763, also a record for that number of qualifiers.

Danny Sullivan would be allowed to be first in the original qualifying line on Sunday, because Guerrero's car ran out of fuel after his late run, delaying time trials.

"Danny, through no fault of his own, would not have had enough fuel for the run he started," said USAC Chief Steward Tom Binford. "We called him in because Guerrero had stopped on course. They went back for fuel and didn't get back until six o'clock, so he goes first tomorrow."

What would the weather bring on Sunday, for Cheever and Michael Andretti to take the final pole shots?

Guerrero had his hopes.

"I hope it's really hot and greasy," Roberto said. "I hope it's horrible."

Top; Al Unser Jr. had to settle for a less than desirable run from his Galmer chassis. Right; Pole sitter Roberto Guerrero was swamped by the media after his record-breaking run.

	Date:	Saturday, May 9
	Weather:	Rain, High 67 degrees
Qualification Attempts:	23	
	Qualifiers:	18

Today's Qualifiers:

Car	Driver	Speed
36	Roberto Guerrero	232.482
2	Mario Andretti	229.503
6	Arie Luyendyk	229.127
51	Gary Bettenhausen	228.932
23	Scott Brayton	226.142
4	Rick Mears	224.594
12	Bobby Rahal	224.158
5	Emerson Fittipaldi	223.607
3	Al Unser Jr.	222.989
91	Stan Fox	222.867
8	John Andretti	222.644
19	Eric Bachelart	221.549
44	Philippe Gache	221.496
10	Scott Pruett	220.464
93T	John Paul, Jr.	220.244
7	Paul Tracy	219.751
48	Jeff Andretti	219.306
15T	Scott Goodyear	219.054
	(Bumped May 17)	

Formulated For A Fast Finish.

For a spectacular look in less time, Glidden Spred Satin® and Spred® House Dura-Flat are formulated to cover the first time, so you can get the job done in less time. Maybe that's why Glidden so quickly became the most preferred brand of interior paint and why over half the households in America have used Glidden.

POWER DRIVE™

Glidden

A better way to paint.™

ICI Paints *World Leader*

Glidden is proud to be the exclusive paint sponsor of the Indianapolis 500® Power Drive.

The speed and good fortune of Roberto Guerrero in setting the pace for the pole on the first qualifying day didn't carry over to King Motorsports teammate Jim Crawford.

Although four drivers and cars still had a pole shot today, including entries for Eddie Cheever and Michael Andretti, Crawford was relegated to second-day qualifier status by a chaotic series of events that he termed a "disaster."

It also turned into a turnabout day for Cheever.

Tony Bettenhausen brought out the caution during the morning practice by slamming the wall in turn #3 after fluid came out of the car's right rear. Bettenhausen was taken to Methodist Hospital for X-rays of a bruised left shoulder.

Then at 10:56 a.m., Cheever pulled out of the pits at the same time Ted Prappas was coming in. The pair collided on pit road and Prappas' machine sustained left front wheel and suspension damage.

"Cheever pulled out in front of me," Prappas said. "I don't think he ever saw me. The crew sent him out right as I went by. I was in the right lane. he should've pulled into the left lane, not out into the fast lane."

"I was waved out by both my crew chief and the official," said Cheever. "When you go out at a 45-degree angle, you leave the pits blind, so Prappas was coming in and I didn't see him. I feel bad, but there were officials in the lane next to me, and there was nothing I could do."

The incident didn't deter Cheever, who hit 230 miles an hour for the first time, registering his best lap of the month at 230.970 miles an hour.

Meanwhile, Crawford's car had another engine failure, and the crew was frantically trying to change engines and get the machine in line as a first-day qualifier.

At 12:05 p.m., five minutes after the start of qualifying, nine crewmen hustled the car to pit road, two of them still working on it and three others carrying bodywork. Crew member Mike Perkins was injured when the front left tire ran over his foot and ankle.

The car didn't make it and A.J. Foyt's machine was pushed to the scales as the first second-day qualifier, leaving Crawford out of the pole position picture.

"They changed it in 40 minutes," Crawford said. "Three hours is good. We were going to

Top; 1985 winner Danny Sullivan qualified for his tenth Indy start. Right; Al Unser Sr., the newest member of the Menard team, qualified for his 26th Indy 500.

finish building it out here. It's a major disaster. We'll have a team of 20 guys back there working to get me out this afternoon."

While this drama was playing itself to a conclusion, Danny Sullivan rolled to the line and became the day's first qualifier. After rookie Jimmy Vasser waved off, Cheever went out and recorded an average of 229.897, good for the middle spot in the front row.

"The car I had today could have done 232 yesterday," Cheever said. "Those were the four hardest laps I've ever run."

He was asked about starting second.

"Yesterday, I would have told you 'no,'" he said, "This morning, 'no.' Those are my best speeds of the month, the four finest laps since I've been here."

Of the first-day qualifiers, Michael Andretti

	Date:	Sunday, May 10
	Weather:	Sunny, High 79 degrees
Qualification Attempts:	11	
	Qualifiers:	9

Today's Qualifiers:

Car	Driver	Speed
9	Eddie Cheever	229.639
26	Jim Crawford	228.859
1	Michael Andretti	228.169
18	Danny Sullivan	224.838
27T	Al Unser	223.744
14	A.J. Foyt, Jr.	222.798
21	Buddy Lazier	222.688
11	Raul Boesel	222.434
47	Jimmy Vasser	218.268

Top; Long time A.J. Foyt supporter Jim Gilmore was pleased to learn that Foyt had qualified for his 35th Indy 500. Left; PPG Director of Racing Jim Chapman rewarded Roberto Guerrero for winning the PPG Pole Award.

Top; With a half hour to go, Jim Crawford finally got his opportunity to become a first weekend qualifier. Bottom; Michael Andretti's hopes for the pole position were dashed by a run that landed him outside of the second row.

was last to go, at 12:13 p.m.

He put together a solid average of 228.169 miles an hour, but it wasn't quite enough for a front-row starting spot. Roberto Guerrero had his first "500" pole, Cheever had his first "500" front-row starting spot and Mario Andretti would start on the outside. The pole Buick would be flanked by a pair of the new Fords.

And it was the first time in Speedway history that three former Formula One drivers had occupied the front row.

Foyt and Vasser qualified in the first hour of activity, bringing the field to 23. The rest waited until the last 1 1/2 hours of the day to seek cooler track temperatures on the front straightaway.

Raul Boesel had replaced Hiro Matsushita in the Dick Simon fleet after Matsushita's injury. He had jumped in the car for the morning practice. But a few hours later, his crew pushed into line at 4:32 p.m. and chalked up a steady average of 222.434 miles an hour to land comfortably in the show.

The "banzai charge" of the last half-hour was led by Crawford, who qualified at 228.859 miles an hour at 5:37 p.m. Instead of a pole or front-row shot, he would start 21st.

"We're done slapping each other on the back and saying, 'Hard luck,'" Crawford said. "We need now to run a race."

Al Unser put the substitute Team Menard car in the race at 223.744. Then came Buddy

Lazier at 222.688 and Fabrizio Barbazza ended the day's qualifying when he brushed the wall in turn #2 on his third lap.

That left 27 cars in the field with a field average of 224.025, almost five miles an hour faster than the comparable 1991 group at this point.

Among those who would wait a week to go for the final six spots were two-time winner Gordon Johncock, veterans Bettenhausen and Didier Theys and rookies Mark Dismore, Prappas, Jeff Wood, Lyn St. James and Jovy Marcelo.

While the on-track activity was commanding the attention, Drs. Terry Trammell and Tom Southern returned Nelson Piquet to surgery to survey wound sites, and found no sign of complications. Piquet was on the mend.

But qualifying had been two days of records and milestones.

Three of the four rookies who qualified on the first weekend - Eric Bachelart, Philippe Gache and Paul Tracy - had beaten the previous record for rookie qualifiers.

Eight former winners were "in." Guerrero's pole was the first for Buick since Pancho Carter in 1985 and it broke a string of five straight Chevy poles at Indy.

One week down, one week to go.

The start of the final week for speed usually has its share of car-hopping, as drivers and teams try to find the right combination to make the field.

This day is more one of deal-making than of track time. But 28 cars went out, many teams starting to try Race Day setups.

The changes started at mid-day when Dale Coyne Racing bought a 1991 Lola/Buick from King Motorsports and announced rookie Brian Bonner as the driver. Bonner had appeared at USAC's Rookie Orientation Program in April, but had not been on the track during the month of May.

Railbirds still figured it would take a 220-mile-an-hour average to make the field. The search for speed would continue, largely by drivers with older cars trying to reach that mark.

It would be difficult. Temperatures, low for the first week, reached a more seasonal 82 degrees on this day and that held speeds down.

Jeff Wood was the fastest of those not-yet-qualified at 216.050. Jovy Marcelo was next at 215.275. It was not a day for an older car to reach 220 miles an hour.

Scott Pruett, at 2:44 p.m. in a Truesports entry, did a 360-degree spin in turn #1 with no contact.

Meanwhile, veteran driver Tero Palmroth told of his appearance the night before as guest conductor of the Indianapolis Symphony Orchestra for a special performance for the relief fund at St. Petersburg (Leningrad) in the former Soviet Union.

"They said the conductor would start and I'd go on and do it for two minutes with the conductor," Palmroth said later. "So I went out and the conductor left me there. I was watching the drummer to see what to do.

"I was more nervous than in qualifying here."

The qualified teams were balancing their ledgers. Guerrero's pole was worth $145,000 in cash and prizes, including the PPG Pole Award of $100,000 cash and a Starcraft/Chevrolet van worth $35,000, and one of the three $10,000 GTE Front

Top; Rookie Jeff Wood was looking for enough speed to make the field on the second weekend. Right; Although Frenchman Philippe Gache was a first weekend qualifier, he continued to log important miles during practice.

Date:	Monday, May 11
Weather:	Sunny, High 82 degrees
Drivers on Track:	22
Cars on Track:	28
Total Laps:	881

Top Five Non-Qualified Drivers of the Day:

Car	Driver	Speed
34	Jeff Wood	216.050
50	Jovy Marcelo	215.275
38	Didier Theys	214.505
92	Gordon Johncock	212.670
66	Mark Dismore	209.527

Runner Awards for a front-row start.

For some, it was on to Race Day. For others, the challenge still loomed.

Frustration continued for those who hadn't qualified for the 1992 Indianapolis 500.

Jovy Marcelo was tops among that group with a speed of 216.534, followed by Didier Theys at 216.247.

Those speeds were still four miles an hour short of what most felt would be necessary to make the 33-car starting lineup.

Rookie Brian Bonner got his first track time of May after talking to the media during a press conference.

His car with Dale Coyne Racing was the machine that Jim Crawford had raced at Indy in 1991.

"The pressure's on with the history of that car and how well it has run," Bonner said, "but it also takes some pressure off because the car is capable of doing those speeds."

The "500" would be Bonner's first-ever oval race.

"I guess I picked a big one," he said, "but I'd rather start here than say, Phoenix or Nazareth."

Meanwhile, figures released on "trap speeds" from USAC Timing and Scoring for the best laps of the top qualifiers to date had many in Gasoline Alley abuzz.

Date:	Tuesday, May 12
Weather:	Overcast, Rain, High 77
Drivers on Track:	20
Cars on Track:	20
Total Laps:	398

Top Five Non-Qualified Drivers of the Day:

Car	Driver	Speed
50	Jovy Marcelo	216.534
38	Didier Theys	216.247
34	Jeff Wood	215.481
92	Gordon Johncock	214.859
66	Mark Dismore	213.680

Guerrero's fastest lap of 232.618 boasted a turn #1 speed of 232, two miles an hour faster than his nearest challenger at that trap, Mario Andretti.

He was also fastest by two miles an hour in turn #2 at 229. The railbird analysis was that Guerrero was really hauling his car through the south end of the race track.

But race day was a new ball game.

Top; Mario Andretti, comfortable in the field took the second week of practice a little lighter. Left; Rookie Brian Bonner got a lot of coaching from car owner Dale Coyne before taking on the Brickyard.

The second week continued on this day with no car/driver combination comfortable which was not already qualified for the 1992 Indianapolis 500.

Ted Prappas was fastest of nine car/driver combination who sought speed in earnest, but hit only 216.388. The speeds ranged from Prappas' clocking to the 210.374 posted by Brian Bonner in his first full day on the 2 1/2-mile oval.

Bonner, in the process of reaching 210, lost two engines in his new Dale Coyne Racing entry and only two days remained before the final qualifying weekend.

The deck continued to shuffle with the announcement that veteran Pancho Carter was named to the backup car of Stan Fox by the Hemelgarn-Byrd Racing stable.

The car had been practiced by Fox at 225.761 miles an hour earlier in the month. Carter, a 17-year veteran, knew his way around at Indy.

"Actually, I have Thursday, Friday, Saturday and Sunday," he said. "I guess I have three days to waste. Stan got the car set up so I really don't think it's a problem whatsoever getting the car up to speed and to qualify."

He was asked his prediction of the slow speed to make the field, and he echoed the same opinion of everyone - - still - along pit road.

"Somewhere around the 220 mark is realistic," he said. "If it gets real, real hot or windy, speeds probably won't come up like the first day of qualifying."

Meanwhile, Lyn St. James, bidding to become only the second woman driver to start the "500," was still having problems with her Dick Simon Racing entry powered by an aging Cosworth.

In practice on May 6, St. James had recorded a lap of 219.796 miles an hour to exceed the world's closed-course speed record for women of 217.498 set by Patty Moise in a Buick Regal on Jan. 23, 1990 at Talladega Superspeedway.

But 219-plus was not enough, and the tired powerplant could only muster 212.988 on this day, sixth among not-yet-qualified car/driver combinations. The looks of frustration were beginning to show.

Al Unser, shaking down his machine for Race Day, had a minor setback when he brushed the wall off turn #4. The car had a broken right front wheel and right front sus-

Above; Veteran Pancho Carter was invited to pilot a Hemelgarn-Byrd ride. Right; Rookie Lyn St. James remained frustrated with her Cosworth powered effort.

Date:	Wednesday, May 13
Weather:	Sunny, Windy, High 75
Drivers on Track:	33
Cars on Track:	34
Total Laps:	1,623

Top Five Non-Qualified Drivers of the Day:

Car	Driver	Speed
31	Ted Prappas	216.388
66	Mark Dismore	215.941
16T	Tony Bettenhausen	215.765
34	Jeff Wood	214.194
90	Lyn St. James	212.988

pension damage.

The Speedway offered incentive to qualifiers on the second, third and fourth days by adding $120,000 in qualifying prizes to be spread among the top three qualifiers on each of those days.

That put $25,000 on the line for the top qualifiers on each day of the final weekend, as well as for Jim Crawford, who turned out to be the fastest second-day qualifier.

At Methodist Hospital, the news also brightened. Nelson Piquet underwent continued skin grafting surgery and was improving. Hiro Matsushita was released.

Only two days remained before the final "showtime" to make the field.

For the first time this week, a car/driver combination not yet qualified reached 220 miles an hour.

Rookie Ted Prappas, who had suffered a setback when his P.I.G. Racing entry was damaged over the weekend in a pit-road collision with Eddie Cheever, topped the charts at 221.212, becoming the only driver to reach the "ball park requisite" that seemed safe to make the field.

Others moved up. Tony Bettenhausen reached 219.904 and Pancho Carter, in his first seat time in the backup Hemelgarn-Byrd car, hit 219.539.

But the big news came from the Dick Simon camp. In a flurry of motion and hurried announcements, rookie Lyn St. James was moved into the backup car of Philippe Gache, a car with the Chevy V/8A powerplant.

Ford Motor Co., for which St. James was under contract as a product development consultant and marketing spokesperson, announced that she "was free to compete in any car."

Formula Project, the French consortium which was involved with Simon to field the cars for Gache, gave its blessing. And St. James went out, saddled up in the backup and ran 218.140.

"We're still working on her primary car (with Cosworth power)," Simon said. "The problem is a turbocharger and engine compat-ibility situation. We're finding things to try. No other decision will be made until you see what (car) goes out to the qualifying line."

Preparations continued well for some, not so well for others. Brian Bonner passed his driver's test. But Jeff Wood, struggling for speed, spun and hit the wall in turn #4 and the car sustained right-side damage. Wood escaped with a bruised left knee.

On the sidelines, Bobby Rahal's crew led by Jim Prescott nailed down the final spot in the semifinal round of the $51,000 Miller Genuine Draft Indy 500 Pit Stop Contest. The team changed two tires in a record 11.186 seconds, breaking its own mark of 11.298 set in the 1991 preliminaries.

Date:	Thursday, May 14
Weather:	Cloudy, Rain, High 67
Drivers on Track:	29
Cars on Track:	31
Total Laps:	1,126

Top Five Non-Qualified Drivers of the Day:

Car	Driver	Speed
31	Ted Prappas	221.212
16T	Tony Bettenhausen	219.904
81	Pancho Carter	219.539
44T	Lyn St. James	218.140
50	Jovy Marcelo	216.878

Above; Speedway veteran Tony Bettenhausen continued to search for the reason for his slow month. Left; Hard-working Emerson Fittipaldi logged 1,570 practice miles for the Marlboro backed Penske team.

"One thing you learn in racing is that they don't wait for you." *Roger Penske*

When he was 14 years old, Roger Penske's father took him to see his first Indianapolis 500. He hasn't missed one since. "The crowd, the excitement—it just got to me," he recalls. "That's when I said to myself, 'Someday I'm going to compete here.'"

Eighteen years later he made it to Indy as the leader of Team Penske— "a group of drivers, engineers, and mechanics who were as committed to the challenge of racing as I was." To date, Team Penske has won eight Indy 500 victories, making it the most successful team ever.

In addition to managing his racing team, Penske runs an international multibillion-dollar automotive business. Whatever his endeavor, he uses the same management techniques. "I try to teach my people

that it's up to them to innovate, to make things happen. You can't just sit around and wait."

In his work, Roger Penske combines a strong focus on results with attention to detail. "The thing I like about Rolex," he explains, "is that they don't compromise either. If you're going to do something, you might as well be the best at it. That's why I've worn a Rolex for over two decades."

ROLEX

Some drivers practiced at speeds which looked comfortable to qualify, but tragedy struck on the day before the final time trial weekend.

Rookie Jovy Marcelo went into turn #1 at 4:07 p.m., did a three-quarter spin and hit the outside wall. His Euromotorsport Fendi AGIP Taumarin IEMA Slam entry slid to a stop in turn #2.

Marcelo was unconscious when rescue workers reached him, and he was pronounced dead of head injuries on arrival at 4:35 p.m. at Methodist Hospital.

The young Filipino became the first driver to lose his life at the Speedway since Gordon Smiley in 1982.

Tony Bettenhausen led the pack of those still waiting to qualify with an average speed of 221.033 miles an hour. Didier Theys was next at 220.146, followed by Dominic Dobson in the Burns Racing/Tobacco Free America entry at 220.060.

The figure 220 was still the benchmark, but others were close. Pancho Carter reached

Left; Johnny Parsons, attempting to make the field for the first time since 1986, carried some inspiration along in the cockpit. Below; Rookie Ted Prappas prepped for a second weekend attempt.

219.577 and Mike Groff worked with the primary Mackenzie Financial machine from the Walker Motorsports garage at 218.755.

Lyn St. James upped her speed in the Chevy-powered backup to Philippe Gache to 218.733.

Other drivers jumped into cars. Rocky Moran was announced in a Team Menard backup. Fabrizio Barbazza switched to a Euromotorsport entry. And veteran Johnny Parsons climbed aboard the Arciero Racing machine vacated by Barbazza.

Also off the track, USAC outlined "Item H" of its supplementary regulations for the race, which stated that "the pits will be closed when the yellow light first appears and will not be reopened until a pack-up has been established."

Strategy to accommodate the new rule - or take advantage of it if opportunity presented itself - was discussed up and down pit road.

The procedure, which was installed in the interest of safety, created a new twist.

Nelson Piquet's feet and ankles continued to improve.

Above; Mike Groff was prepared to put a second Mackenzie car into the field. Right; First weekend qualifier Buddy Lazier was idle while his car went through an overhaul.

Date:	Friday, May 15
Weather:	Sunny, High 78 degrees
Drivers on Track:	31
Cars on Track:	33
Total Laps:	1,413

Top Five Non-Qualified Drivers of the Day:

Car	Driver	Speed
16T	Tony Bettenhausen	221.033
38	Didier Theys	220.146
68	Dominic Dobson	220.060
81	Pancho Carter	219.577
15T	Mike Groff	218.755

"Everything's going like clockwork," said Dr. Terry Trammell. "There were many potential complications, none of which has occurred yet. There aren't any problems at this point."

Qualifying beckoned.

If it works on the track,

it'll work on the road.

There's no more hostile environment on earth for a spark plug than on a race track. Yet Champion Spark Plugs were the choice of more Indy 500 winners than all other brands combined.

No wonder Champion is the world's number 1 selling spark plug for family cars as well.

CHAMPION ®

NO MATTER WHAT YOU DRIVE.

As the bustle began around Gasoline Alley, 1983 winner Tom Sneva hustled to the Hanna Medical Center to become the 51st driver to take his physical.

From there, he went to the Menard garage and replaced Rocky Moran in the team's back-up machine. Moran had been assigned to the car only 24 hours. Although Moran turned a few laps in the Menard machine, he decided to vacate it because of an uncomfortable cockpit. "Car hopping" had reached full blossom.

When qualifications opened at 11:04 a.m., Pancho Carter rolled away from the starting line and took a lap at 214.720 miles an hour, but waved off. Didier Theys was next, but waved off after laps of 219.689 and 218.277.

It was hot, and speeds suffered. Highs today would reach 84 degrees. Ted Prappas warmed up the P.I.G. Racing entry, but didn't take the green.

Then came Lyn St. James, with history and a frustrating month on her shoulders.

She had reached 219-plus in practice in the backup Chevy-powered machine from the Dick Simon stable. The questions were if it was enough, or if more was needed.

St. James started marginally. Her first circuit was 218.585. But she increased her speed on each of her four laps to 221.119 on the final, and a 220.150 average, exactly what bystanders and drivers alike predicted was needed to make the field.

"I just wanted that checkered flag," St. James said. "This was no time to start thinking. I didn't experience any emotions. I called to the crew that the car was perfect. They put their blood, sweat and skin into the car. I wanted to share that with them, that the car was perfect.

"When I came down pit lane and saw everyone clapping, I knew we were in. I'm still rather numb. It wasn't until an interview that I knew we were faster than other cars that had qualified."

Thus, St. James became the second woman to qualify at Indy, and the oldest rookie at 45.

Brian Bonner followed with a strong run at 220.845, making the 29-car field average a healthy

223.778. Others would wait for cooler temperatures late in the day.

But practice continued. At 4:42 p.m., Pancho Carter's month ended just three days after it started when the left front suspension snapped as he entered the second turn. He hit the wall hard with the right side and slid down the backstretch, suffering a broken right arm.

After Dominic Dobson waved off a run to start "Happy Hour" at 5:05 p.m., Mike Groff, in the Walker Motorsports machine, left the pits for an attempt, but the yellow came on for debris before he could start a run. He chose to wait.

It was a time of strategy in the Walker pits. Scott Goodyear had qualified the team's back-up 1991 Lola/Chevy Indy V/8A on the first weekend at 219.054 and the team thought it

Above; Armed Forces Day ceremonies are a tradition during the second weekend of qualifying. Right; Indianapolis Mayor Stephen Goldsmith enjoyed the day with his daughters Elizabeth and Olivia.

	Date:	Saturday, May 16
	Weather:	Sunny, High 84 degrees
Qualification Attempts:	9	
	Qualifiers:	3

Today's Qualifiers:

Car	Driver	Speed
15	Mike Groff	221.801
	(Car driven in race by Scott Goodyear)	
39	Brian Bonner	220.845
44T	Lyn St. James	220.150

might not be enough.

The idea for the weekend was to put Groff in the 1992 Lola primary machine, get it qualified, and hope both speeds would hold up. If both stood, then the drivers would switch cars and both would start on the end of the 33-car field. If Goodyear was bumped, he would take over Groff's qualified car.

So whatever Groff did, his car was the one that needed to be clearly fast enough, or Walker Motorsports could be shut out. Johnny Rutherford was available in a third machine, but not up to speed.

Groff waited until 5:39 p.m., and reeled off four steady laps for a 221.801 average. The strategy worked...for the moment.

"I'm really happy about it all," Groff said. "Derrick Walker gave me the chance. He (Goodyear) set the car up and I went out and drove it."

It turned out to be the last successful attempt of the day, as Sneva and Gordon Johncock waved off on later runs.

Thirty cars were now in the field, three spots were open and 13 driver/car combinations were waiting in the wings for judgment day on their fates in the field.

Top; Pancho Carter made contact with the turn two wall during practice and ended his bid for an 18th Indy start. Below; Lyn St. James, under new Chevrolet power became only the second woman to qualify for the Indy 500.

DAY 16
SUNDAY, MAY 17

When qualifying opened for the final day, the last-chance qualifiers were ready.

Some were prepared to take slower speeds and pray for rain or other miracles. Others would gut it out to the end, waiting for the precise moment to make their runs, hoping to squeeze every ounce of speed out of their mounts.

Rookie Kenji Momota was first up for TEAMKAR, in a 1991 Lola/Chevy V/8A acquired from Galles-Kraco Racing. His average was 218.967, second slowest of the 31 qualifiers.

After waveoffs by Mark Dismore in the Comet Kart Sales Lola/Buick and Johnny Parsons in the ALFA-LAVAL Lola Buick, Dominic Dobson took out the Burns Racing/Tobacco Free America Lola Chevy V/8A.

Gordon Johncock bumped Jimmy Vasser to make way for his 24th Indy start.

The car was a 1991 model driven in the 1991 edition of the "500" by Al Unser, Jr. The Burns team had turbocharger problems the day before, necessitating the wait until the final day. Dobson turned in an average of 220.359, although he started with a 221-plus lap and ended at 218-plus.

"We had a Lola Buick but really wanted a Chevy," Dobson said. "That didn't come around until Thursday p.m. We didn't get up to speed until Friday and we lost boost, so we gambled."

Dobson was the day's only qualifier until 2:45 p.m. Tom Sneva, who had waved off twice previously, took a chance on his final strike in the Menard/Glidden/Conseco Lola Buick and checked in at 219.737.

Sneva's run filled the field and bumping would be next. Jimmy Vasser was first up on the bump list at 218.268. Sneva strung together some one-liners about his run. They went something like this:

Q: Your thoughts about a last-minute qualifying attempt...

SNEVA: It's obviously not related to a high IQ.

Q: Why did John Menard choose you?

SNEVA: I was the last guy standing in the parking lot.

Q: Did you think you were going to have a ride this year?

SNEVA: I was almost gonna hafta be nice to Foyt.

Q: What adjustments did you make to the car?

SNEVA: The hardest part is trying to fit in (Gary) Bettenhausen's seat..that's not exactly a

classic body style.

Q: You've said before that you don't see well - how is your eyesight now?

SNEVA: The best thing I learned from Foyt is the psychology of racing. I'd wear different glasses for different things. I'd wear these big thick ones for the drivers' meeting and trip all over everything.

After a waveoff by Tony Bettenhausen and a "no go" by Johnny Parsons, Gordon Johncock rolled out the STP/Jack's Tool Rental/ Hemelgarn 1991 Lola Buick at 3:50 p.m.

The two-time winner put the car in the show at a four-lap average of 219.288, bumping Vasser from the field. Johncock's qualification gave the field a record 10 former winners with a record 20 wins among them.

For Johncock, it was a long, hard month.

"I'm not going to lie to you," he said. "A couple of times, I felt like going home, especially after blowing an engine first thing this morning. I'll be gone (back to the farm in Michigan) in an hour or two, whenever this thing is over. I need to grind some feed for the steers. They've been out since Wednesday."

Vasser's bump was short-lived. Just 12 minutes later, Vasser put his backup machine on the line and averaged 222.313 to knock out Momota and put Scott Goodyear on the bubble.

"We've been prepared for this all week long," Vasser said. "We worked with the 'T' car all week because we knew something like this was bound to happen. It's been the longest week of my life going over all the different scenarios of what could possibly happen."

From there, it was an hour's wait.

Didier Theys was first to go of the "Happy Hour" group at 5:15 p.m. in the Pennzoil Special Lola Chevy V/8A which had been qualified for the 1991 race by John Andretti.

But his first lap was only 214.230 and the machine spewed smoke down the front straightaway on the second, ending his bid.

Tony Bettenhausen, on his third attempt, waved off after two laps. Parsons waved off after one, Dismore after three.

With six minutes left in qualifying, Ted Prappas went out for his third and final attempt in the P.I.G. Racing entry. His four-lap average was 219.173, just .119 of a mile-an-hour fast enough to make the field.

His speed was still the slowest of the 33 starters, immediately putting him in bump position for one final attempt which would be

	Date:	Sunday, May 17
	Weather:	Cloudy, High 80 degrees
Qualification Attempts:		17
Qualifiers:		6

Today's Qualifiers:

Car	Driver	Speed
47T	Jimmy Vasser	222.313
	(Bumps K. Momota, #88, 218.967)	
68	Dominic Dobson	220.359
59	Tom Sneva	219.737
92	Gordon Johncock	219.288
	(Bumps J. Vasser, #47, 218.268)	
31	Ted Prappas	219.173
	(Bumps S. Goodyear, #15T, 219.054)	
88	Kenji Momota	218.967
	(Bumped by J. Vasser)	

made by three-time winner Johnny Rutherford.

Rutherford rolled away in the Macklanburg-Duncan Lola Chevy V/8A with a minute left, but his four laps averaged only a bit more than 217.

Prappas was in, at the fastest slow speed in history, almost six miles an hour faster than Johncock's slowest speed of 1991.

"This was the worst two weeks of my life and now it's the best five minutes of my life," Prappas said. "Our car seems to like cool, cloudy days. It doesn't like sunshine. This worked. I can just start breathing again."

The field average was a record 223.479, nearly five miles an hour faster than 1991.

And it was on to Race Day.

Top; Johnny Rutherford made a last minute attempt to place a second Derrick Walker prepared car in the field. Left; Ted Prappas nudged Scott Goodyear from the field with the fastest slow speed in the history of the Indianapolis 500.

CARBURETION DAY
THURSDAY, MAY 21

Above; Eddie Cheever surveyed the Carburetion Day crowd. Right; Mario Andretti and Eddie Cheever went head to head in the semi finals of the Miller Pit Stop Contest. Bottom; Pit Stop Contest winner Bobby Rahal gave his crew a hand with the equipment.

The traditional "Carburetion Day," the final time for teams to practice, can be two hours of encouragement or two hours of problems.

Teams had been "off" the track for three days, and this final period would be "it" until the starting command was given on Race Day.

It was here that the new Ford Cosworths showed what they could do, with Race Day setups and full fuel loads.

The four Fords were atop the speed standings, with Mario Andretti leading the way at 226.409, followed by Arie Luyendyk at 225.423, Michael Andretti at 225.220 and Eddie Cheever at 224.921.

"We're where we wanted to be," said Mario. "All we can do now is hope for the best."

"It doesn't surprise me at all," said Luyendyk. "We've been fastest all month except for the Buicks. Being fast on Carb Day isn't all that important but it's nice to have a psychological edge on the competition."

Seven uneventful caution flags delayed the practice, for debris and tow-ins. All 33 starters participated and Mike Groff practiced in the first alternate position.

"Mike will serve as first alternate," Derrick

Top; Al Unser Jr. fine tuned his Chevrolet during practice. Bottom left; Mario Andretti was the fastest on Carb Day. Bottom Right; Rick Mears reports back to his boss Roger Penske after the morning practice session.

49

Walker said while officially selecting a driver for the car after Scott Goodyear swapped into the field. "It's either Mike or me and I'll let him take care of that."

Chief Steward Tom Binford issued a bulletin to competitors that set a speed limit of 100 miles an hour on pit road during the race, a measure added to previous new pit procedures.

And Bobby Rahal's team, headed by Jim Prescott, captured the 16th annual Miller Genuine Draft Indy 500 Pit Stop Contest with a clocking of 13.324 seconds for a four-tire change, beating the Chip Ganassi Racing entry of Arie Luyendyk.

Michael Andretti had been first on the track for the final practice and Dominic Dobson had been the last of the 33 starters to practice.

Now all bets were off. Race Day was next.

Date:	Thursday, May 23
Weather:	Rain, Windy, High 80
Drivers on Track:	34
Cars on Track:	34
Total Laps:	840

Top Five Drivers of the Day:

Car	Driver	Speed
2	Mario Andretti	226.409
6	Arie Luyendyk	225.423
1	Michael Andretti	225.220
9	Eddie Cheever	224.921
36	Roberto Guerrero	224.899

Becky Reinhold from
Lexington, Kentucky,
breaks the ribbon to win the
Women's Division of the
16th Annual 500 Festival
"Minnie" Marathon.

500 FESTIVAL

Clockwise from right: Disney entertained at the Mayor's Breakfast; From L to R: Katherine Ashton, Rebecca Springer, 500 Festival President Steve Stitle, Queen Mary Troyer, Amy Held and Angela Smith; Dawn Costelow proudly displays her Festival of the Arts Grand Award; 1992 500 Festival Parade Grand Marshal Mickey Mouse; Festival Queen Mary Troyer greeted the Opening Day crowd.

53

OS/2

Starting today, everything your computer has ever done, it will do better.

You've created documents, crunched numbers, even conquered alien invaders. Still, your software hasn't really been able to make the most of your hardware. But now it can.

Introducing OS/2® 2.0. It's a new way to take your computer programs beyond the limitations of the past—it lets you do more with them than you ever could with DOS or DOS with Windows.™

It's also a way to run more than one program at a time. Print a document and calculate a spreadsheet while you open files, for example. You can even "cut and paste" between *any* programs—drop text from WordPerfect® 5.1 into a Lotus® 1-2-3® for Windows spreadsheet—the possibilities are endless.

About the only thing better than how much more OS/2 lets you do, is how easily it lets you do it all. Friendly icons fill the screen—even installation is graphically guided. And OS/2 comes with **HelpWare**™ a range of services and support, including a toll-free number. But maybe the best part is that instead of buying DOS, Windows and Adobe Type Manager™ you get them all with OS/2.

With OS/2, your software can catch up with your hardware. And you can do the only thing you haven't been able to do with your computer. Make the most of it. For an IBM authorized dealer near you, or to order OS/2 2.0—at special introductory prices of $49 for Windows users and $99 from any DOS—call 1 800 3-IBM-OS2.*

Introducing OS/2 2.0.

– *Runs programs made for DOS, Windows and OS/2.*
– *Runs more than one program at a time so you don't waste time.*
– *Easy to install, learn and use. Has online help and tutorial.*
– *Makes the most of 386 SX hardware and above.*
– *OS/2 2.0 upgrade: $49 from Windows, $99 from any DOS.***

WINNER
AL UNSER JR.

#3 Valvoline Galmer '92 Chevrolet
Entrant: Galles-Kraco Racing   Crew Chief: Owen Snyder

Starting Position:	12
Qualifying Average:	222.989 MPH
Qualifying Speed Rank:	14
Best Practice Speed:	228.055 MPH
Total Practice Laps:	646
Number Practice Days:	14
Finishing Position:	1
Laps Completed:	200 134.477 MPH
Highest Position 1992 Race:	1
Fastest Race Lap:	196 223.981 MPH
1992 Prize Money:	$1,244,184
INDY 500 Career Earnings:	$2,645,624
Career INDY 500 Starts:	10
Career Best Finish:	1

*F*or Al Unser Jr, the month started out with frustration.

On Day #2, his car blew an engine and oil and water dripped into the cockpit.

"Blew a hole in it," Unser Jr, said. "It got hot in the seat. I tried to get it back to the pits but it finally got unbearable."

While Buicks and Fords chased after the pole, Unser Jr, with Chevy Indy V/8A power, qualified at a "modest" 222.989, good for 12th starting spot.

"When I went out this morning, the car was loose," he said. "The car was working well, but it was still a little loose through the corner on that first lap.

Had the car been 'right' this morning, the delay wouldn't have made a difference, but we're just hit and miss on setups."

On Race Day, he was in the hunt, but Michael Andretti clearly held the edge until dropping out, setting up the now-storied battle between Unser Jr, and Scott Goodyear, which ended in the closest finish in Indy history (.043).

"I was looking for the white flag on lap #198," Unser Jr, said. "I thought this was the infamous last lap that I've always wanted to lead. But from the time we went green from that last yellow, I never let up."

2nd PLACE
SCOTT GOODYEAR

#15 MacKenzie Financial Special
Entrant: Walker Motorsports, Inc.   Crew Chief: Buddy Lindblom

Starting Position:	33
Qualifying Average:	221.801 MPH
Qualifying Speed Rank:	21
Best Practice Speed:	224.321 MPH
Total Practice Laps:	547
Number Practice Days:	14
Finishing Position:	2
Laps Completed:	200 134.477 MPH
Highest Position 1992 Race:	2
Fastest Race Lap:	197 224.624 MPH
1992 Prize Money:	$609,333
INDY 500 Career Earnings:	$859,094
Career INDY 500 Starts:	3
Career Best Finish:	2

*S*cott Goodyear's month of May was his first with Walker Motorsports and, although the team hoped for a good finish, there was no run for the pole.

He qualified his backup car, a 1991 Lola/Chevy V/8A, on Pole Day at 219.054, slowest of the 21 first-day qualifiers.

"We had a little problem with the main car," Goodyear said. "I decided to run the 'T' car because 23 minutes into the session, I had a little motor mishap. So I wanted to put this car in the show."

Later, it was decided to let Mike Groff qualify the '92, and, if Goodyear was bumped, swap drivers. Groff got in at an average of 221.801, and Goodyear was bumped six minutes from the end of qualifying. He swapped with Groff and started 33rd.

At the start, Goodyear moved up rapidly. He was seventh at 50 miles, fell a lap behind once, but charged back. When Michael Andretti fell out, there was Goodyear, on the tail of leader Al Unser Jr.

On lap #197, he turned his fastest lap of the race, at 224.624, almost three miles an hour faster than he had traveled all month.

Goodyear gathered in Unser Jr, to set up the storybook finish, closest in Speedway history.

"They tell me that we missed winning by 43/1000ths of a second," he said. "I only wish the start-finish line had been 100 yards down."

3rd PLACE
AL UNSER

#27 Conseco Special

Entrant: Team Menard, Inc.   Crew Chief: Joe Kennedy

1992 LOLA/BUICK

Starting Position:	22
Qualifying Average:	223.744 MPH
Qualifying Speed Rank:	12
Best Practice Speed:	224.372 MPH
Total Practice Laps:	150
Number Practice Days:	7
Finishing Position:	3
Laps Completed:	200 134.375 MPH
Highest Position 1992 Race:	1
Fastest Race Lap:	112 223.292 MPH
1992 Prize Money:	$368,533
INDY 500 Career Earnings:	$3,183,148
Career INDY 500 Starts:	26
Career Best Finish:	1

*F*or Al Unser, May started out just as it did when he won his fourth "500," in 1987 — on the sidelines.

The elder Unser was without a ride, and prospects for a competitive seat didn't seem good.

But on Day #6, Nelson Piquet crashed and was out for the month. Car owner John Menard turned to the veteran to pilot the Piquet backup, a 1992 Lola/Buick.

With little practice, Unser put the machine in the race three days later at a four-lap average of 223.744 miles an hour.

"I would have liked to have more time," Unser said. "The crew and the car are capable of faster speeds. But I wanted to put it in the show today, so I have to be careful because I don't have another car.

For the race, he started 22nd. He picked off traffic steadily until cracking the top 10 just before the 200-mile mark, a lap down at that point.

But he unlapped himself and eventually led for four laps, increasing his all-time Speedway career record to 629.

With 75 miles remaining, he was fourth behind Michael, Scott Goodyear and Al, Jr. When Michael dropped out, Unser finished third to give the Buick engine its best-ever result.

"It's really great to have the race that we had and then to have your boy win it," Unser said. "That's neat."

4th PLACE
EDDIE CHEEVER

#9 Target-Scotch Video Lola Ford Cosworth
Entrant: Chip Ganassi Racing Teams, Inc.   Crew Chief: Chris Griffis

1992 LOLA/FORD

Starting Position:	2
Qualifying Average:	229.639 MPH
Qualifying Speed Rank:	2
Best Practice Speed:	230.971 MPH
Total Practice Laps:	579
Number Practice Days:	13
Finishing Position:	4
Laps Completed:	200 134.374 MPH
Highest Position 1992 Race:	1
Fastest Race Lap:	40 226.273 MPH
1992 Prize Money:	$271,103
INDY 500 Career Earnings:	$579,480
Career INDY 500 Starts:	3
Career Best Finish:	4

*F*or Eddie Cheever, starting on the front row at Indianapolis was a surprise.

After a pit road accident with Ted Prappas on the morning he qualified, Cheever practiced at more than 230 miles an hour and qualified at 229.639.

"Yesterday, I would have told you 'No,'" he said. "This morning, 'No.' Now I'm elated. Those are my best speeds of the month, the four finest laps since I've been here."

He was asked how he felt about being on the front row.

"I don't know quite yet," he said. "I haven't walked up and seen what it looks like from there."

On Race Day, he stayed right with the leaders, seldom falling out of the top five before losing a lap near the 300-mile mark. He led three times for nine laps.

He bemoaned what he called the "stop-and-go" nature of the race.

"It wasn't a race," he said. "It was stop and go and stop and go and in and out. Our tires were so cold today that it was hard to get any temperature into them.

"There are two pedals in a race car. The one on the right goes fast, the one on the left stops. It's your choice how fast you want to go."

5th PLACE
DANNY SULLIVAN

#18 Molson/Kraco/STP Galmer '92 Chevrolet
Entrant: Galles-Kraco Racing   Crew Chief: Paul Harcus

Starting Position:	8
Qualifying Average:	224.838 MPH
Qualifying Speed Rank:	9
Best Practice Speed:	225.383 MPH
Total Practice Laps:	579
Number Practice Days:	14
Finishing Position:	5
Laps Completed:	199 Running
Highest Position 1992 Race:	5
Fastest Race Lap:	197 222.294 MPH
1992 Prize Money:	$211,803
INDY 500 Career Earnings:	$1,733,553
Career INDY 500 Starts:	10
Career Best Finish:	1

*D*anny Sullivan spent one of his quietest months in the early going at Indianapolis, although it was louder than in 1991, when he struggled with Alfa Romeo power.

He was back with a Chevy in the new Galmer chassis for Galles-Kraco and soldiered it into the field at 224.838 miles an hour as an original line qualifier.

Although it was 7 1/2 miles an hour slower than Roberto Guerrero's pole speed, Sullivan's run was the fastest of any driver with Chevy Indy V/8A power.

And he started eighth — the same spot from which he claimed victory at Indy in 1985.

"Except for the last lap, all of them were faster than I've been all month," Sullivan said of his run. "It's nice to be first in class."

On Race Day, he bided his time, falling out of the top 10 by the 100-mile mark and re-emerging later. At the end, he moved from seventh to fifth.

"I'm very happy with the finish," he said. "If you would have asked me before the race I would have been happy with fifth. In the middle of the race, I would have been happy with a top 10 finish."

THE COLD YOU CAN'T CATCH.

With Bobby Rahal at the controls of the Miller Genuine Draft® Indy car, other drivers will be doing more chasin' than racin'.
Cold-Filtered™ Miller Genuine Draft. Get Out Of The Old. Get Into The Cold.

6th PLACE
BOBBY RAHAL

#12 Miller Genuine Draft Special
Entrant: Rahal/Hogan Racing, Inc.   Crew Chief: James Prescott

1992 LOLA/CHEVY

Starting Position:	10
Qualifying Average:	224.158 MPH
Qualifying Speed Rank:	11
Best Practice Speed:	228.432 MPH
Total Practice Laps:	751
Number Practice Days:	16
Finishing Position:	6
Laps Completed:	199 Running
Highest Position 1992 Race:	2
Fastest Race Lap:	147 225.564 MPH
1992 Prize Money:	$237,703
INDY 500 Career Earnings:	$2,000,166
Career INDY 500 Starts:	11
Career Best Finish:	1

*B*obby Rahal had been consistent through the early part of the 1992 season, taking the PPG Cup point lead to Indianapolis.

He was serving in a new role as a co-car owner as well as a driver, and the purchase by himself and Carl Hogan of the former Patrick team's assets was a new experience.

During the month, he stayed almost anonymously in and around the top 10 in the daily speed standings. Eventually, he qualified at 224.158 for 10th spot, second to Danny Sullivan among Chevy Indy V/8A drivers.

It was the most consistent qualifying run in Speedway history, the times on the four laps being just .006 of a second apart.

"I'm pleased with our speed and especially the consistency," he said. "I think it will be a very good and consistent car during the race. I know the owner is pleased with the driver right now."

On Race Day, he settled in for the long haul, but ran as high as second in the middle stages. A flat right rear hampered his effort.

"A flat right rear tire really hurt us today," he said. "I could run in front of Al Jr. and the rest of the Chevy cars, but I lost a lap when the tire went down. That one flat tire cost us a chance to win.   We're still leading the points and going to Detroit in one piece."

1992 LOLA/CHEVY

#11 Panasonic/SEGA Lola

Entrant: Dick Simon Racing, Inc.

Crew Chief: Mike Albrecht

Starting Position:	25
Qualifying Average:	222.434 MPH
Qualifying Speed Rank:	19
Best Practice Speed:	222.750 MPH
Total Practice Laps:	157
Number Practice Days:	4
Finishing Position:	7
Laps Completed:	198 Running
Highest Position 1992 Race:	7
Fastest Race Lap:	176 221.893 MPH
1992 Prize Money:	$191,503
INDY 500 Career Earnings:	$930,665
Career INDY 500 Starts:	6
Career Best Finish:	3

*R*aul Boesel's month started by looking for a ride. He was looking to return to the 33-car starting lineup after a year's absence and a third-place finish in 1990.

Although he had talked to Dick Simon Racing about a car, he didn't get his hands on one until Hiro Matsushita broke his right thigh in a crash during practice on Pole Day morning and Simon called on him in a relief role.

The next morning, Boesel practiced for the first time and qualified it at 4:32 p.m. that day at 222.434 for 25th starting position.

"I'm pleased with it," he said. "I didn't expect to qualify this weekend, but when we saw the speeds come up, we thought, 'Well, let's go.' That's the fastest I've ever gone here and the car ran beautifully."

As attrition took its toll and Boesel picked his way through the pack, he reached the top 10 by the 300-mile mark. He finished seventh, two laps off the pace.

"The hardest part of the race was to keep concentration and not let down because of all the long yellows," he said. "The car ran like a clock all day...no problems whatsoever. It was a really fine race for me."

8th PLACE
JOHN ANDRETTI

#8 Pennzoil Special

Entrant: Hall/VDS Racing   Crew Chief: David Brzozowski

1992 LOLA/CHEVY

Starting Position:	14
Qualifying Average:	222.644 MPH
Qualifying Speed Rank:	18
Best Practice Speed:	228.920 MPH
Total Practice Laps:	665
Number Practice Days:	14
Finishing Position:	8
Laps Completed:	195 Running
Highest Position 1992 Race:	6
Fastest Race Lap:	193 223.686 MPH
1992 Prize Money:	$186,203
INDY 500 Career Earnings:	$720,882
Career INDY 500 Starts:	5
Career Best Finish:	5

*J*ohn Andretti looked to be a "sleeper."

He had been in the top 10 in the speed standings for six of the seven days leading up to Pole Day and figured to be a contender for the top spots.

But he waved off after three laps in the 221 mile-an-hour bracket on his qualifying attempt in his backup car and put his primary in 14th starting spot at 222.644.

"I was nowhere near what I wanted," he said. "The whole purpose of being here is to do your best. What we did today was trying to do our best. We have a couple of small prob-lems that turn into major problems at 220."

On Race Day, his car proved to be sixth fastest of all the starters, with a circuit of 223.686 on lap #193. On one pit stop, though, he slid sideways into the pits, losing time.

His finish of eighth was his second-best in five Indy appearances.

"Today would have been a golden opportunity," he said. "I came into the pits too hard and bumped the pit wall, bending the front wing and steering arm. We lost too many laps trying to fix it. There was nobody I could look at but myself."

Copenhagen®

You can't miss Copenhagen
in the PPG Indy/CART Series...and
you can't miss with the great taste of
Copenhagen, the leader in moist smokeless
tobacco satisfaction.

9th PLACE
A.J. FOYT, JR

#14 A.J. Foyt/Copenhagen Racing
1992 LOLA/CHEVY
Entrant: A.J. Foyt Enterprises   Crew Chief: Craig Baranouski

Starting Position:	23
Qualifying Average:	222.798 MPH
Qualifying Speed Rank:	16
Best Practice Speed:	226.695 MPH
Total Practice Laps:	229
Number Practice Days:	10
Finishing Position:	9
Laps Completed:	195 Running
Highest Position 1992 Race:	9
Fastest Race Lap:	195 216.118 MPH
1992 Prize Money:	$189,883
INDY 500 Career Earnings:	$2,637,963
Career INDY 500 Starts:	35
Career Best Finish:	1

*Q*ualifying was a different story for A.J. Foyt in 1992.

In 1991, he had been "first out" when the track opened for time trials and he put his car on the front row.

But as the last potential qualifier on 1992's first day, he pulled in after three laps in the 226 mile-an-hour bracket. He was first up after the original qualifying line and checked in at 222.798 for 23rd spot on the grid.

"Not really very good at all," he said after the run. "The car was pushing real bad in (turns) 3 and 4. How the right rear didn't kiss it (the wall), I'll never know,

but I'd hate to have had my fingers in there.

"I'll have to be very cautious (in the race) because from where I'll be starting, there's about a 25 percent chance that I could be in an accident."

On Race Day, although five laps down, he finished ninth after outlasting problems.

"I'm just glad to finish this race," he said. "Considering everything, it went pretty good. We should've been in about three or four wrecks. We got behind on the first yellow when I ran over debris from (Tom) Sneva's accident. It bent something in front 'cause you can see where the thing (car) is towed out a mile."

Choice of the Indianapolis 500

The world-renowned Indianapolis 500 auto race is rich in history and nostalgia.

It's no wonder they have, once again, chosen Starcraft as their exclusive luxury van

conversion. Starcraft was founded in 1903 and continues to produce products with

integrity and of the highest quality standards. And Starcraft luxury vehicles are

known worldwide as the industry leader. So if you are looking for a world-class driving

experience, own a Starcraft. It is destined to be a classic.

The World-Class Choice

STARCRAFT ◢◤®

10th PLACE
JOHN PAUL, JR

#93 D.B. Mann Development Buick
Entrant: D.B.Mann Motorsports, Inc.   Crew Chief: Dave Hoffpauir

1990 LOLA/BUICK

Starting Position:	18
Qualifying Average:	220.244 MPH
Qualifying Speed Rank:	27
Best Practice Speed:	221.926 MPH
Total Practice Laps:	462
Number Practice Days:	13
Finishing Position:	10
Laps Completed:	194 Running
Highest Position 1992 Race:	9
Fastest Race Lap:	193 214.367 MPH
1992 Prize Money:	$171,403
INDY 500 Career Earnings:	$520,931
Career INDY 500 Starts:	4
Career Best Finish:	10

*J*ohn Paul, Jr., made progress in 1992, starting with qualifying on the first day.

He averaged 220.244 on his four-lap qualifying run in a two-year-old Lola with Buick power, good for 18th on the grid, his best Indy start in four outings.

"I'm extremely happy," he said. "It was the first time I've done it on the first day. I'm going to enjoy the next three days of qualifying. It's fantastic...a real relief. We'll live with it. I think it's safe."

With a two-year-old car, Paul would be cautious on Race Day. But for the last 150 miles, although he was six laps down at the end, he was in the top 10.

His 10th-place finish was his career best at Indy, but Paul said it could've been better.

"We broke a fuel cable before the race," he said, "so we had to replace it before the start. Then the car wouldn't idle and it was stalling in the pits. Under yellows in traffic, it would stall and I'd have to bump start it. But the Buick finished the race."

Bank One Salutes

LYN ST. JAMES
Ft. Lauderdale, Florida

Winner of the
1992 Bank One
Indianapolis 500
Rookie of the Year
Award

11th PLACE
LYN ST. JAMES

#90 Agency Rent-A-Car/JCPenney "Spirit of the American Woman"   1991 LOLA/CHEVY
Entrant: Paragon Motorsports, Inc.   **Crew Chief: Gerry Cook**

Starting Position:	27
Qualifying Average:	220.150 MPH
Qualifying Speed Rank:	28
Best Practice Speed:	221.533 MPH
Total Practice Laps:	592
Number Practice Days:	14
Finishing Position:	11
Laps Completed:	193 Running
Highest Position 1992 Race:	11
Fastest Race Lap:	169 211.810 MPH
1992 Prize Money:	$187,953
INDY 500 Career Earnings:	$187,953
Career INDY 500 Starts:	1
Career Best Finish:	11

*L*yn St. James started the month of May with an eye on history.

She would try to become the first woman since Janet Guthrie to make the field, and the first to try since Desire Wilson in the early '80s.

Her effort, in a 1991 Lola/Cosworth, was stymied through most of the month by turbocharger problems with the now-vintage powerplant.

But a backup machine for Philippe Gache in the Dick Simon stable with a Chevy Indy V/8A motor became available, and she traveled faster on her qualifying run than she had on previous practice days to record a four-lap average of 220.150.

"For the first time since I was allowed to get on to the race track, I was able to use the revs," Lyn said.

About her place in history, she added, "I'm proud to be a woman, I'm proud to be a driver. I'm glad I wasn't the first."

On Race Day, she had a conservative plan. It would be her first championship race. She dodged accidents all day long to register an 11th-place finish.

"At the beginning, I made a couple of moves and I wasn't successful on them," she said. "It was like, 'Darn' and I settled down. I kept cool so we just did it. The car was absolutely perfect all day."

12th PLACE
DOMINIC DOBSON

1991 LOLA/CHEVY

#68 Burns Racing/Tobacco Free America
Entrant: Burns Racing Team, Inc.   Crew Chief: Tom Bloom

Starting Position:	29
Qualifying Average:	220.359 MPH
Qualifying Speed Rank:	26
Best Practice Speed:	221.675 MPH
Total Practice Laps:	190
Number Practice Days:	5
Finishing Position:	12
Laps Completed:	193 Running
Highest Position 1992 Race:	11
Fastest Race Lap:	39 213.008 MPH
1992 Prize Money:	$179,983
INDY 500 Career Earnings:	$676,752
Career INDY 500 Starts:	5
Career Best Finish:	12

*D*ominic Dobson's program with Burns Racing came together late in the month.

When the team got its Chevy Indy V/8A engine, Dobson popped into the third spot in the speed standings for not-yet-qualified drivers the day before the final qualifying weekend at a speed of 220.060 miles an hour.

On the third qualifying day, he waved off after two laps, but put the year-old Lola in the show on the last day at 220.359. His last lap, though, dropped to 218-plus.

"I was scared to death of hitting the wall if I went too fast," he said. "The car had a bad push on laps two and three. So I backed off on lap four because I felt I had a good average and I didn't want to lose the car."

On Race Day, he worked his way from 29th starting position to 12th at the end, seven laps off the pace, to claim the final PPG Cup championship point.

"I feel pretty good," he said. "We finished. I got docked laps for passing under the yellow. The car didn't handle well in traffic, but I didn't practice here in traffic, so I didn't know what to expect. I'm glad we finished, considering where we started."

13th PLACE
MICHAEL ANDRETTI

#1 Kmart/Texaco Newman/Haas Lola Ford Cosworth   1992 LOLA/FORD
Entrant: Newman/Haas Racing   Crew Chief: Thomas Wurtz

Starting Position:	6
Qualifying Average:	228.169 MPH
Qualifying Speed Rank:	7
Best Practice Speed:	232.013 MPH
Total Practice Laps:	390
Number Practice Days:	14
Finishing Position:	13
Laps Completed:	189 Fuel Pressure
Highest Position 1992 Race:	1
Fastest Race Lap:	166 229.118 MPH
1992 Prize Money:	$295,383
INDY 500 Career Earnings:	$1,850,305
Career INDY 500 Starts:	9
Career Best Finish:	2

*M*ichael Andretti's fortunes in the 1992 Indianapolis 500 belied the skills of he and the Newman/Haas team.

He was steadily on the leader board in the search for speed leading up to Pole Day, reaching 232 miles an hour with the new Ford Cosworth engine.

But he drew a high number in the batting order for qualifying, and when rain delayed the line, he was forced to qualify in the heat of the second day in a bid for the pole.

He put the car in the show at 228.169 miles an hour, good only for sixth starting spot.

"It was very frustrating," he said. "I knew the conditions were dynamite yesterday. The car was capable of getting the pole if I had had the power that I had before. It had the balance to get it done."

His Race Day strategy was simple, as he started behind his father, Mario.

"I need Dad to stand on it and I need to stand on him from behind," he said. "I want to get up there quick."

On Race Day, he did just that, leading the first lap. In all, he led 160 laps and dominated the race before fuel pressure problems sidelined him in 13th.

"It can't get much worse than this," he said. "This place is cruel, so cruel."

14th PLACE
BUDDY LAZIER

#21 Leader Cards Lola
Entrant: Leader Cards, Inc.   Crew Chief: John Barnes

Starting Position:	24
Qualifying Average:	222.688 MPH
Qualifying Speed Rank:	17
Best Practice Speed:	223.220 MPH
Total Practice Laps:	338
Number Practice Days:	11
Finishing Position:	14
Laps Completed:	139 Blown Engine
Highest Position 1992 Race:	14
Fastest Race Lap:	126 211.924 MPH
1992 Prize Money:	$164,283
INDY 500 Career Earnings:	$326,973
Career INDY 500 Starts:	2
Career Best Finish:	14

*B*uddy Lazier came into the month of May with a new team (Leader Cards) and a year-old car that had been driven by Danny Sullivan in the 1991 edition of the "500."

The car had run the previous year with an Alfa Romeo powerplant, but the team had put in a Buick for '92.

When qualifying opened, Lazier was fifth out, but waved off after three laps in the 218-219 bracket.

He made the field on his second attempt at 222.688, more than four miles an hour faster than Sullivan had qualified in it the year before.

"Actually, we were running really well yesterday morning," Lazier said of his aborted first-day try. "We had a few mechanical problems which caused us to lose about 10 miles an hour on the straightaway."

On Race Day, he lasted 139 laps before a blown engine ended his run.

"We'd been working all day to get up there," he said. "The car was starting to run really good. Right in between (turns) one and two, I felt the motor go and the oil just started pouring in. I said (to chief mechanic John Barnes), 'John, it's starting to get hot,' and he said to get out of there."

15th PLACE
ARIE LUYENDYK

#6 Target-Scotch Video Lola Ford Cosworth   1992 LOLA/FORD
Entrant: Chip Ganassi Racing Teams, Inc.   Crew Chief: Steve Melson

Starting Position:	4
Qualifying Average:	229.127 MPH
Qualifying Speed Rank:	4
Best Practice Speed:	232.654 MPH
Total Practice Laps:	440
Number Practice Days:	11
Finishing Position:	15
Laps Completed:	135 Crash
Highest Position 1992 Race:	1
Fastest Race Lap:	135 223.170 MPH
1992 Prize Money:	$166,953
INDY 500 Career Earnings:	$2,090,534
Career INDY 500 Starts:	8
Career Best Finish:	1

*A*rie Luyendyk became the fourth Ford driver when he was assigned to the second car for Chip Ganassi Racing, and he made his mark.

The 1990 winner joined the 230-mile-an-hour club during practice and was the first qualifier when the track opened on Pole Day after a rain delay.

He put track record numbers on the board, setting one-lap marks of first 228.967, then 229.305 before chalking up a record average of 229.127.

"I'm just really glad to get this out of the way," he said. "Going out second or third is better. Going out first, you don't know if there are any changes in the track.

"If it doesn't hold for the pole, I'll be happy on the front row. If it doesn't hold for the front row, I'll be disappointed."

Later runs put him fourth in the starting lineup.

On Race Day, he ran with the front runners and led lap #48 before an accident sidelined him after 135 laps. He was second to Michael Andretti just before the crash.

"It was a typical racing accident," he said. "I went below one of the backmarkers and as I was beside him, he didn't see me, so he came down on me and forced me way down on the apron. When I went down into turn #4, I bottomed out with the front end, it pushed the wheel off the ground and I had no steering."

1991 LOLA/CHEVY

#31 Say No to Drugs/P.I.G. Racing
Entrant: Norman C. Turley   Crew Chief: John Weland

Starting Position:	32
Qualifying Average:	219.173 MPH
Qualifying Speed Rank:	33
Best Practice Speed:	221.212 MPH
Total Practice Laps:	385
Number Practice Days:	12
Finishing Position:	16
Laps Completed:	135 Gear Box
Highest Position 1992 Race:	9
Fastest Race Lap:	59 213.934 MPH
1992 Prize Money:	$163,253
INDY 500 Career Earnings:	$163,253
Career INDY 500 Starts:	1
Career Best Finish:	16

*F*or Ted Prappas, making his first Indianapolis 500 field was dramatic, and a welcome 180-degree turn from his first try in 1991.

The previous year, Prappas had crashed twice. But this time, he overcame a pit-road accident with Eddie Cheever during practice for Pole Day qualifying to make the show.

He didn't have a lot of time to spare.

Two days before the final qualifying weekend, he took the No. 1 spot among drivers not-yet-qualified with a lap at 221.212 miles an hour. A run at the end of the third day and a second on the fourth day were waved off.

With six minutes remaining in time trials, Prappas rolled off the line for his third and final attempt, and nudged his way into the field with a four-lap average of 219.173, barely bumping Scott Goodyear. He was elated.

"I'm gonna be happy for the rest of my life," he said. "This has been the worst two weeks of my life and now it's the best five minutes of my life."

In the race, he lasted 135 laps before gearbox failure left him in 16th. He had one narrow escape, going into the grass to dodge the spinning cars of Rick Mears and Jim Crawford.

"Something in the gearbox," he said after bowing out. "That's all I know."

17th PLACE
GARY BETTENHAUSEN

#51 Glidden Paints Special
Entrant: Team Menard, Inc.   **Crew Chief: Darrell Soppe**

1992 LOLA/BUICK

Starting Position:	5
Qualifying Average:	228.932 MPH
Qualifying Speed Rank:	5
Best Practice Speed:	229.317 MPH
Total Practice Laps:	625
Number Practice Days:	16
Finishing Position:	17
Laps Completed:	112 Crash
Highest Position 1992 Race:	4
Fastest Race Lap:	43 220.550 MPH
1992 Prize Money:	$150,803
INDY 500 Career Earnings:	$1,174,794
Career INDY 500 Starts:	20
Career Best Finish:	3

*G*ary Bettenhausen, in his third year with Team Menard, looked to have a good shot for the front row with a new Lola and Buick power.

He was the only driver other than Roberto Guerrero to be in the top 10 of the speed charts for each of the first seven days of practice.

When it became time to qualify, he racked up track records for turbocharged stock-block engines with a fastest lap of 229.317 and a four-lap average of 228.932.

It was good for the middle of the second row.

"The weather had something to play in it," Bettenhausen said. "The car wasn't turning as good a numbers as this morning. The humidity hurts this thing. It's not the hat in terms of horsepower."

On Race Day, he hovered steadily in the middle of the top 10 before an accident involving Jeff Andretti put him out for the day in 17th.

"He (Andretti) crashed and hit the wall," Bettenhausen said. "There was debris everywhere and all I could do was try to weed my way through it. One of his wheels went up about 30 feet in the air and crashed down on my left front suspension."

A true artiste should be known for his inspiration, not perspiration.

18th PLACE
JEFF ANDRETTI

#48 Gillette/Carlo/Texaco/Copenhagen
Entrant: A.J. Foyt Enterprises   Crew Chief: Mark Scott

1991 LOLA/CHEVY

Starting Position:	20
Qualifying Average:	219.306 MPH
Qualifying Speed Rank:	31
Best Practice Speed:	223.375 MPH
Total Practice Laps:	482
Number Practice Days:	14
Finishing Position:	18
Laps Completed:	109 Crash
Highest Position 1992 Race:	16
Fastest Race Lap:	109 212.109 MPH
1992 Prize Money:	$153,703
INDY 500 Career Earnings:	$321,193
Career INDY 500 Starts:	2
Career Best Finish:	15

*J*eff Andretti didn't have a ride for the PPG Cup trail for 1992, but arranged with A.J. Foyt to pilot his second car for the month of May in a bid for a second "500" start.

When time trials opened, he was the fourth qualifier and the second of the four Andrettis to make the show.

His average of 219.306 was second slowest among 21 first-day qualifiers, but it was good enough.

"I'm safe with this time," he said. "It's not as good as I wanted it. The car was starting to go away but it's a fairly decent spot."

The 28-year-old youngest member of the Andretti clan talked about his advice from Foyt.

"To run consistent and drive it to the limit," Jeff said. "Dad was very elated for me when A.J. offered the ride. It's an honor to run for A.J. at the Speedway."

On lap #110 of the race, Andretti went into turn #2 and hit the outside wall hard. He suffered broken bones in both lower legs, ankles and feet and underwent lengthy surgery at Methodist Hospital.

"It's a terrible thing that happened," said Foyt. "What caused the accident was the right rear hub broke. It was not where the wheel came off where somebody didn't tighten it. The hub broke itself. It just makes me sick when someone gets hurt in one of my cars."

1991 LOLA/BUICK

#39 Applebee's/Danka

Entrant: Dale Coyne Racing   Crew Chief: Doug Myers

Starting Position:	26
Qualifying Average:	220.845 MPH
Qualifying Speed Rank:	24
Best Practice Speed:	221.255 MPH
Total Practice Laps:	327
Number Practice Days:	7
Finishing Position:	19
Laps Completed:	97 Crash
Highest Position 1992 Race:	7
Fastest Race Lap:	38 209.351 MPH
1992 Prize Money:	$156,953
INDY 500 Career Earnings:	$156,953
Career INDY 500 Starts:	1
Career Best Finish:	19

*B*rian Bonner started his month of May in the middle.

He got a ride in a Dale Coyne Racing entry after Coyne acquired a 1991 Lola from King Motorsports, a car Jim Crawford had driven at the Speedway in 1991.

From there, Bonner passed his driver's test just two days before the final qualifying weekend and was the second qualifier of the third day at an average speed of 220.845 miles an hour.

It was a whirlwind effort for his first Indy Car start.

"I'm a little surprised," he said. "I picked up a couple of miles an hour since practice. It's a lot easier going fast around the track than going slow. It's pretty scary going slow. When I came by the white flag, I kept thinking, 'Don't screw up now, you're going pretty good.'"

It was good enough for 26th in the starting line-up. In the race, he stayed out of trouble until a restart that began lap #103. He spun and hit the outside wall in turn #4, but was uninjured.

"I'm not sure what happened," Bonner said. "The car just got away from me. I didn't lose it. Based on what I heard, I would guess I was helped."

20th PLACE
PAUL TRACY

#7 Mobil 1 Penske Chevy '91
Entrant: Penske Racing, Inc.   Crew Chief: Tim Bumps

Starting Position:	19
Qualifying Average:	219.751 MPH
Qualifying Speed Rank:	29
Best Practice Speed:	223.586 MPH
Total Practice Laps:	843
Number Practice Days:	13
Finishing Position:	20
Laps Completed:	96 Failed Engine
Highest Position 1992 Race:	8
Fastest Race Lap:	42 218.957 MPH
1992 Prize Money:	$160,053
INDY 500 Career Earnings:	$160,053
Career INDY 500 Starts:	1
Career Best Finish:	20

*F*or Paul Tracy, getting the chance to qualify at Indianapolis for the Penske team was a culmination of his year-long testing contract.

He had been signed by Penske as a test driver in 1991, and would get his shot in the team's third car this month of May.

Tracy's effort had a setback on Day #4, when he came out of the pits, got sideways in turn #1 and hit the wall with the right side, with the result of heavy right side and nose damage to the machine.

But on Pole Day, he was ready, and qualified another Penske entry at 219.751 miles an hour, good for 19th starting spot.

"I don't think people realize how young I am," he said after qualifying for his first "500."

"I'm 23 years old but I've been racing since I was eight. Being involved with Chevrolet, Penske, Mobil...it's just unbelievable. Everybody on the team trusts my judgment. They don't come over and force-feed me."

Even though he started back in the pack, Tracy moved up to reach the top 10 in the early stages, reaching eighth at one point.

However, engine failure ended his day after 96 laps.

"The motor went away," Tracy said. "It was running great. We were taking our time and gaining positions. In a matter of time, we would've been in the top three."

21st PLACE
JIMMY VASSER

1991 LOLA/CHEVY

#47 Kodalux/Hayhoe-Cole
Entrant: Hayhoe-Cole Racing, Inc.   Crew Chief: Mike Hull

Starting Position:	28
Qualifying Average:	222.313 MPH
Qualifying Speed Rank:	20
Best Practice Speed:	222.844 MPH
Total Practice Laps:	488
Number Practice Days:	13
Finishing Position:	21
Laps Completed:	94 Crash
Highest Position 1992 Race:	12
Fastest Race Lap:	53 215.131 MPH
1992 Prize Money:	$170,853
INDY 500 Career Earnings:	$170,853
Career INDY 500 Starts:	1
Career Best Finish:	21

*J*immy Vasser had his ups and downs in his first month of May at Indianapolis.

On Day #1, he was 10th fastest out of 30 cars on the track at 218.978 miles an hour. On his first qualifying attempt in the original line, he waved off after a lap at 216.554. But he took the checkered flag on his second attempt with a 218.268 average.

"I haven't run in conditions like this all month," he said. "My qualifying run is the first I've had to run where the track was a little warmer. We decided to go ahead and put it in the show."

He had to do it twice. Gordon Johncock bumped him from the field at 3:50 p.m. on the final time-trial day. But Vasser went out 12 minutes later and bumped Kenji Momota from the show with a run of 222.313.

"We've been prepared for this all week long," he said. "We put ourselves through a crash course in 'bubblism.' I've had about as much of the bubble as I can stand."

On Race Day, he went out in an accident after 94 laps, hitting the turn #1 wall. He underwent surgery at Methodist Hospital for a broken right thigh.

His month of May ended in 21st place.

22nd PLACE
SCOTT BRAYTON

#22 Amway-Northwest Airlines
Entrant: Dick Simon Racing, Inc.   **Crew Chief: Mark Bridges**

Starting Position:	7
Qualifying Average:	226.142 MPH
Qualifying Speed Rank:	8
Best Practice Speed:	227.848 MPH
Total Practice Laps:	473
Number Practice Days:	11
Finishing Position:	22
Laps Completed:	93 Blown Engine
Highest Position 1992 Race:	2
Fastest Race Lap:	42 221.538 MPH
1992 Prize Money:	$173,683
INDY 500 Career Earnings:	$1,256,149
Career INDY 500 Starts:	11
Career Best Finish:	6

*S*cott Brayton and his Dick Simon Racing team faced decisions through the early part of the month of May.

The biggest one was whether to use Chevy Indy V/8A or Buick power. The team had Lolas fitted for each.

On the month's fourth day, though, the Buick question had a setback when Brayton hit the turn #4 wall.

"It looks like we made our decision," he said.

However, the car was deemed repairable, and Brayton qualified on the first day at 226.142 miles an hour, good for seventh starting spot.

"This is the first run I've done with four quick laps together," he said. "The decision (on engines) was made this morning. There's great potential in this car. This is the car I definitely want to go with."

After 93 laps on Race Day, though, engine failure struck, relegating Brayton to 22nd place in the standings.

"I was trying to get around (Bobby) Rahal and I was pulling some really good revs," he said. "I was getting a little too much tow off Rahal as I was trying to pass him. The biggest thing is that it's so cold today the oil and water temperatures keep coming down. We were having a time keeping the temp in the motor."

87

1992 LOLA/FORD

#2 Kmart/Texaco Newman/Haas Lola
Entrant: Newman/Haas Racing   Crew Chief: Carl Dean

Starting Position:	3
Qualifying Average:	229.503 MPH
Qualifying Speed Rank:	3
Best Practice Speed:	233.203 MPH
Total Practice Laps:	528
Number Practice Days:	12
Finishing Position:	23
Laps Completed:	78 Crash
Highest Position 1992 Race:	1
Fastest Race Lap:	39 220.621 MPH
1992 Prize Money:	$156,633
INDY 500 Career Earnings:	$2,314,466
Career INDY 500 Starts:	27
Career Best Finish:	1

*M*ario Andretti makes an annual habit of starting the month of May fast.

He was fourth fastest on the second day of practice at 224-plus miles an hour, jumped five miles an hour the next day and hit 231 on the fifth. The day before Pole Day, he reached 233.202, the day's best effort.

Just seven minutes before the close of time trials on the first qualification day, he reeled off an average of 229.503. Although others trailed him in the original qualifying line, it would hold up for his seventh career and second straight front-row starting berth.

"If at all possible, we wanted to get in today and we're happy that we got in," Mario said. "I'm not happy with the speed. I felt that yesterday, when I went 233, laps in the 30s should have been available, but today I knew it would be tough."

On Race Day, his son, Michael, passed him for the lead on the first lap, but he stayed right behind. However, he made two pit stops in the first 11 laps under caution, falling behind in the serial and eventually losing ground.

On the restart after the sixth caution flag, Andretti spun and hit the outside wall in turn #4, ending his day in 23rd place. He underwent surgery at Methodist Hospital to repair broken toes on both feet.

24th PLACE
EMERSON FITTIPALDI

#5 Marlboro Penske Chevy 92
Entrant: Penske Racing, Inc.   Crew Chief: Rick Rinaman

1992 PENSKE/CHEVY

Starting Position:	11
Qualifying Average:	223.607 MPH
Qualifying Speed Rank:	13
Best Practice Speed:	226.729 MPH
Total Practice Laps:	639
Number Practice Days:	13
Finishing Position:	24
Laps Completed:	75 Crash
Highest Position 1992 Race:	3
Fastest Race Lap:	34 219.823 MPH
1992 Prize Money:	$138,703
INDY 500 Career Earnings:	$2,589,300
Career INDY 500 Starts:	9
Career Best Finish:	1

*I*n earlier years, Emerson Fittipaldi was one of the "rabbits" who put up big numbers in early practice.

But in 1992, he didn't reach the top 10 until Day #6, getting into the picture at 225.886 miles an hour. It was faster than his track record of 225.575 set in 1990 qualifying, but slower than other contenders.

For time trials, Fittipaldi became the 11th qualifier of the month, checking in at 223.607 in his new Penske machine powered by the Chevy Indy V/8B engine. By the time he made the run, his two-year-old track record was gone.

"I am very disappointed with my speed," he said. "The target was 225. This year Chevy is taking a quieter role. It's a little bit of a surprise to me. The car handled beautiful. I just needed a little more power."

Fittipaldi started 11th in the race, but was 8th after one lap and sixth after 10 circuits. He was third after 60 laps and moving fast.

But Jim Crawford and Rick Mears tangled in turn #2 and Fittipaldi came on the scene and crashed after the initial mishap. The accident left the 1989 winner with a puncture wound to his left knee and 24th in his ninth start at Indianapolis.

KENNY BERNSTEIN AND QUAKER STATE EXPLODE SIX MYTHS ABOUT MOTOR OIL.

MYTH: Small, higher revving engines run hotter than V-6s and V-8s.

FACT: Not so. Engine temperatures depend more on the number of accessories an engine must run, vehicle weight and driving conditions. Quaker State motor oils are specially engineered to run cool in *all* size engines.

MYTH: A 20W-50 motor oil is the best grade for smaller engines.

FACT: Wrong. General Motors, Ford, Chrysler and most imports do not recommend this weight for late model cars or light trucks. A 20W-50 oil can't flow fast enough to protect adequately at lower temperatures. In addition, 20W-50 oils do not conserve fuel. While Quaker State makes an excellent 20W-50 product, we recommend 5W-30, 10W-30 and 10W-40 for most vehicles.

MYTH: You can't mix brands of motor oil.

FACT: Nonsense. All high quality brands can be mixed. There is no harm in changing to Quaker State if you use another brand. In fact, we'd love it.

MYTH: You shouldn't switch between a conventional motor oil and a synthetic.

FACT: It won't hurt. You can switch between a conventional motor oil like Quaker State 10W-30 and a good synthetic like Quaker State's Synquest™ at any oil change. Conventionals and synthetics are so compatible you can even mix them together.

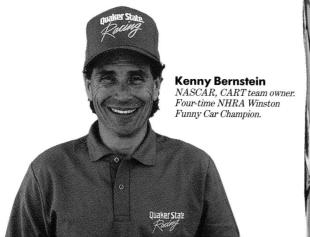

Kenny Bernstein
*NASCAR, CART team owner.
Four-time NHRA Winston
Funny Car Champion.*

MYTH: Motor oils can cause sludge.

FACT: Quality API SG/CD motor oils, like Quaker State, don't cause sludge. Sludge deposits are formed from a combination of dirt, soot and condensed water vapor produced during combustion. The major cause of sludge is not changing oil frequently enough to remove these harmful contaminants. Quaker State motor oils are specially formulated to prevent sludge. Quaker State oils have a unique formula of additives that help to keep dirt and soot particles in suspension until the oil is changed. No other motor oil does a better job of preventing sludge than Quaker State.

MYTH: Paraffinic-based oils can cause wax buildup and sludge.

FACT: Not true. All high quality petroleum motor oils are made from paraffinic-based oils. In spite of its name, paraffin does not mean wax. The stability of paraffin molecules makes paraffin-based motor oils more resistant to the chemical changes that can take place in an engine than other types of crude oils. That means less sludge, varnish and corrosive wear with a high quality paraffin-based motor oil like Quaker State.

QUAKER STATE IS ONE TOUGH MOTOR OIL.

DON'T POLLUTE. PLEASE DISPOSE OF USED MOTOR OIL AND PACKAGING PROPERLY.

©1992 Quaker State Corporation.

25th PLACE
JIM CRAWFORD

#26 Quaker State Buick/King Motorsports
Entrant: King Motorsports   Crew Chief: John Anderson

1992 LOLA/BUICK

Starting Position:	21
Qualifying Average:	228.859 MPH
Qualifying Speed Rank:	6
Best Practice Speed:	233.433 MPH
Total Practice Laps:	348
Number Practice Days:	12
Finishing Position:	25
Laps Completed:	74 Crash
Highest Position 1992 Race:	8
Fastest Race Lap:	41 221.136 MPH
1992 Prize Money:	$167,503
INDY 500 Career Earnings:	$877,463
Career INDY 500 Starts:	7
Career Best Finish:	6

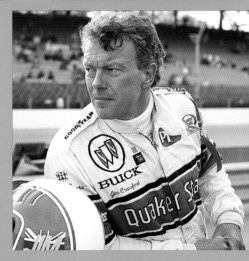

*J*im Crawford may have more testing miles at Indy than any current driver, while doing development work for the Buick Indy V6 engine.

So it was no surprise when he and King Motorsports teammate Roberto Guerrero took turns putting big numbers on the board in the practice session leading up to Pole Day.

Crawford took the top spot, reeling off a lap of 233.433 miles an hour at 5:53 p.m. on May 4, the third day of practice, for the fastest lap in Speedway history. He said he did it without a "tow."

On Pole Day, though, a morning engine failure left Crawford parked as others shot for the No. 1 starting spot, despite heroic efforts by his crew to change the engine in time. He was the fastest second-day qualifier at 228.859, but would start 21st.

"We're going to go 100 percent (during the race)," he said, "the same way we attacked qualifications. We're going to go 100 percent from the start."

By the 10th lap, he had gained 11 places and cracked into the top 10. He had moved to eighth by the 100-mile mark.

But after completing 74 laps, Crawford spun and tangled with Rick Mears in turn #2, putting him out for the day with a broken left foot. His teammate, Guerrero, had failed to take the green flag.

"Rough day, huh?," said car owner Kenny Bernstein. "We don't like it and it's not fun."

1992 PENSKE/CHEVY

#4 Marlboro Penske Chevy 92

Entrant: Penske Racing, Inc.   Crew Chief: Richard Buck

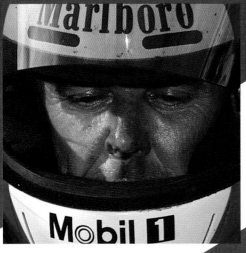

Starting Position:	9
Qualifying Average:	224.594 MPH
Qualifying Speed Rank:	10
Best Practice Speed:	226.273 MPH
Total Practice Laps:	491
Number Practice Days:	12
Finishing Position:	26
Laps Completed:	74 Crash
Highest Position 1992 Race:	10
Fastest Race Lap:	42 218.978 MPH
1992 Prize Money:	$136,403
INDY 500 Career Earnings:	$4,299,392
Career INDY 500 Starts:	15
Career Best Finish:	1

*R*ick Mears' month of May started with hopes of a fifth Indy victory, but setbacks hampered his chances.

Mears had crept into the top 10 on three days of the first week of practice while working with the new Penske chassis and Chevy Indy V/8B engine before a chilling accident on Day #5 left his car on its side in the second turn.

Mears took a trip to Methodist Hospital with a minor fracture in his left foot and a sprained right wrist, but returned to the track two days later.

He qualified at 224.594 miles an hour on the first day of time trials, good for ninth starting spot.

"The guys busted their tails this week and I'm really proud of them," he said of the quick turn-around. "I made a 50 percent gain in the last day. I felt great once I got in the car. You forget about everything else and just concentrate on the qualifying run."

On Race Day, he tangled with a spinning Jim Crawford after 74 laps, putting him out for the day in 26th place, his lowest finish since 1981.

He was released from Methodist Hospital after treatment of a small laceration to his right knee.

27th PLACE
STAN FOX

#91 Jonathon Byrd's Cafeteria/Bryant Heating & Cooling/WMCC
1991 LOLA/BUICK

Entrant: Hemelgarn/Byrd Racing   Crew Chief: Robert Hatch

Starting Position:	13
Qualifying Average:	222.867 MPH
Qualifying Speed Rank:	15
Best Practice Speed:	226.877 MPH
Total Practice Laps:	316
Number Practice Days:	12
Finishing Position:	27
Laps Completed:	63 Crash
Highest Position 1992 Race:	15
Fastest Race Lap:	58 221.011 MPH
1992 Prize Money:	$136,683
INDY 500 Career Earnings:	$670,759
Career INDY 500 Starts:	5
Career Best Finish:	7

*S*tan Fox started the month of May in his second season with the Hemelgarn-Byrd Racing team and a chance for a high starting position.

His car was the last 1991 Lola built, and he pushed it to seventh quickest in practice on the third day of the month.

For qualifying, he safely made the field at a four-lap average of 222.867 miles an hour for 13th starting spot, his best in five "500s."

"I didn't run a lot of laps before qualifying," Fox said. "I don't want something to happen before I qualify. I don't like to take that risk. We made a major change on the rear wing right before qualifying and it worked out great.

"I think we'll do real well," he added. "We have a nicely balanced race car. It's been the smoothest month I've ever had."

His race ended early when he roared through the south short chute only to find Philippe Gache's stricken machine across the track. Fox hit the nose cone of Gache's mount, narrowly avoiding a broadside collision, and his day was over.

"I'm fine," he said. "It's just unfortunate. A car hit the wall — Philippe, I think — I just couldn't get it pulled down in time."

1991 LOLA/CHEVY

#44 Formula Project-Rhone Poulenc Rorer

Entrant: Formula Project/Dick Simon Racing, Inc.   Crew Chief: Greg Beck

Starting Position:	16
Qualifying Average:	221.496 MPH
Qualifying Speed Rank:	23
Best Practice Speed:	224.809 MPH
Total Practice Laps:	413
Number Practice Days:	11
Finishing Position:	28
Laps Completed:	61 Crash
Highest Position 1992 Race:	26
Fastest Race Lap:	25 217.470 MPH
1992 Prize Money:	$136,128
INDY 500 Career Earnings:	$136,128
Career INDY 500 Starts:	1
Career Best Finish:	28

*P*hilippe Gache's first earnest look at an Indy Car came in USAC's Rookie Orientation program.

Gache came to Dick Simon Racing from France, trying to become the first from his country to make a "500" field since Rene Lebegue and Rene Dreyfus co-drove a machine in the 1940 edition of the race.

The rookie became comfortable almost instantly and was the second qualifier of the month at an average speed of 221.496, good for 16th spot on the grid.

"I'm happy because it's wonderful that I qualified," he said, "but I'm also disappointed because I went faster yesterday. During the past week, I was confident about my speeds because they kept going up. I did a 225 yesterday and when I saw the 221 on the dash today, I was disappointed."

His Race Day became frustrating early. He spun in turn #4 prior to the green flag and went to the pits misfiring, in need of a spark-box change. He rejoined the field on lap #3.

Gache completed his 61st lap before spinning and hitting the wall in the south short chute, then was broadsided by Stan Fox, who couldn't avoid his wrecked machine.

"I'm not sure what happened," he said. "I saw a car under heavy braking. I spun and hit the wall and another car hit me."

He was 28th in his first start at Indy.

29th PLACE
GORDON JOHNCOCK

#92 STP/Jack's Tool Rental/Hemelgarn   1991 LOLA/BUICK
Entrant: Hemelgarn/Runyan Racing   Crew Chief: Chris Paulsen

Starting Position:	31
Qualifying Average:	219.288 MPH
Qualifying Speed Rank:	32
Best Practice Speed:	219.673 MPH
Total Practice Laps:	554
Number Practice Days:	14
Finishing Position:	29
Laps Completed:	60 Blown Engine
Highest Position 1992 Race:	18
Fastest Race Lap:	59 213.782 MPH
1992 Prize Money:	$136,003
INDY 500 Career Earnings:	$1,767,601
Career INDY 500 Starts:	24
Career Best Finish:	1

*T*wo-time winner Gordon Johncock, unlike 1991, was ready to go when the month of May started.

He was back with the Hemelgarn team and had two cars at his disposal. But getting up to speed proved to be a struggle. The day before the final weekend of time trials, his best lap was only 216.201 miles an hour.

On the third day of qualifications, he waved off after three laps in the 216-217 bracket, setting up a day of reckoning in the final session.

But he gained the necessary speed, reaching a four-lap average of 219.288 to bump Jimmy Vasser from the field just two hours and 10 min-utes before time trials closed.

Johncock said it was his toughest month at Indy in 20 years. "In 1972 with McLaren, when Peter Revson and I blew seven engines, I didn't qualify till the last day and on my last chance," he said. "Since then, this is the worst month, if I remember right."

He started in the last row (31st) for the second straight year, but unlike his sixth-place finish in 1991, engine failure ended his day early in 29th position.

"I went into turn #2, heard the engine, looked back in my mirror, smoke was coming out, it blew up and that's all," Johncock said dejectedly.

1992 TRUESPORTS/CHEVY

#10 Budweiser Eagle Truesports 92C
Entrant: Truesports Company   Crew Chief: Dennis Swan

Starting Position:	17
Qualifying Average:	220.464 MPH
Qualifying Speed Rank:	25
Best Practice Speed:	224.047 MPH
Total Practice Laps:	531
Number Practice Days:	11
Finishing Position:	30
Laps Completed:	52 Blown Engine
Highest Position 1992 Race:	14
Fastest Race Lap:	38 217.928 MPH
1992 Prize Money:	$143,503
INDY 500 Career Earnings:	$443,747
Career INDY 500 Starts:	3
Career Best Finish:	10

*S*cott Pruett came to Indianapolis with high hopes for continued success with the Truesports chassis, an updated version of the "Made in America" machine debuted in 1991.

He had, for the first time at Indy, a Chevy Indy V/8A engine in the new version of the Truesports, but he wasn't able to crack into the list of pole challengers.

He qualified the first day at a four-lap average of 220.464 miles an hour, nailing down 17th starting position for his third "500."

"We've come a long way since Monday when we had a 206," Pruett said. "Getting around this place

fast takes a lot of experience. I don't know what they were prepared to take for a low speed today. It's a little overwhelming to think that a team will wave off a 220 lap.

"This morning we were trying to get the car set up. We didn't get as much green time as we wanted so I used the first laps of my qualifying run to get the setup better."

In the race, Pruett soldiered his way until engine failure ended his bid after 52 laps with a 30th-place finish.

"Actually, we broke a water line which caused the engine to go," he said. "It was a rough day."

31st PLACE
TOM SNEVA

#59 Menard/Glidden/Conseco Special
Entrant: Team Menard, Inc.   Crew Chief: Jeff Sinden

Starting Position:	30
Qualifying Average:	219.737 MPH
Qualifying Speed Rank:	30
Best Practice Speed:	220.318 MPH
Total Practice Laps:	96
Number Practice Days:	3
Finishing Position:	31
Laps Completed:	10 Crash
Highest Position 1992 Race:	17
Fastest Race Lap:	4 210.709 MPH
1992 Prize Money:	$139,778
INDY 500 Career Earnings:	$1,772,114
Career INDY 500 Starts:	18
Career Best Finish:	1

*T*om Sneva's month started about as late as it could.

He was announced to drive a Team Menard car to replace Rocky Moran on the third morning of qualifications. By late afternoon, he was on a qualifying attempt, though the team waved off after three laps in the 217-mile-an-hour bracket.

In his second attempt the next day, his throttle linkage broke.

That left one final attempt, and on the car's "third strike," he put it in the field at an average of 219.737, joining teammates Gary Bettenhausen and Al Unser.

"There's some real experience in there," he said of his team. "There might be some Geritol in the garage.

"We felt the car was pretty close. It wasn't perfect out there. But we had used up most of the heartbeats this month and didn't want to waste it."

He compared it with his spectacular pole runs of earlier years.

"I don't know if my memory's gone," Sneva said, "but I think there was more pressure today."

On Race Day, his bid was over when he crashed in turn #4 after 10 laps, damaging the left side of the car. He was taken to Methodist Hospital where X-rays were negative, but the 1983 winner's 18th "500" ended in 31st position.

1990 LOLA/BUICK

#19 Royal Oak Charcoal/Mi -Jack
Entrant: Dale Coyne Racing   Crew Chief: Bernie Myers

Starting Position:	15
Qualifying Average:	221.549 MPH
Qualifying Speed Rank:	22
Best Practice Speed:	222.816 MPH
Total Practice Laps:	366
Number Practice Days:	11
Finishing Position:	32
Laps Completed:	4 Blown Engine
Highest Position 1992 Race:	13
Fastest Race Lap:	4 208.121 MPH
1992 Prize Money:	$144,228
INDY 500 Career Earnings:	$144,228
Career INDY 500 Starts:	1
Career Best Finish:	32

*R*ookie Eric Bachelart was one of the month's biggest surprises when qualifying began.

He came to Indianapolis with Dale Coyne Racing for his first "500" bid, and put together a steady qualifying run of 221.549 miles an hour on the first day — eventually becoming the second fastest rookie in the field.

"It feels great," Bachelart said. "You know, when you have a good balance here, it's pretty easy.   It (Indy) is very impressive. After the first turn, you see all these people and then you don't want to look at them. They make you nervous.

"The first time I was here, I did a 222 and I was doing high 222s all week," he added. "I felt confi-

dent. This morning, it was rough (with yellow flags). The Buick engine is strong. We're not struggling at all."

He remained the fastest rookie qualifier until Jimmy Vasser jumped past him while bumping his way back in the field on the final day.

Bachelart started 15th in the lineup but an engine failure caused an early exit.

"Maybe the transmission broke and the engine blew up," he said. "The first lap in traffic, I was watching to make sure all was okay. The time in the race was short...too short....too bad because it went so well, with our qualifying and our whole month."

33rd PLACE
ROBERTO GUERRERO

#36 Quaker State Buick/King Motorsports
Entrant: King Motorsports   Crew Chief: John Anderson

1992 LOLA/BUICK

Starting Position:	1
Qualifying Average:	232.482 MPH
Qualifying Speed Rank:	1
Best Practice Speed:	232.624 MPH
Total Practice Laps:	375
Number Practice Days:	13
Finishing Position:	33
Laps Completed:	0 Crash
Highest Position 1992 Race:	Did Not Start
Fastest Race Lap:	Did Not Start
1992 Prize Money:	$286,378
INDY 500 Career Earnings:	$1,400,842
Career INDY 500 Starts:	8
Career Best Finish:	2

*R*oberto Guerrero and the King Motorsports team were ready for May and he became the first driver ever to turn a practice lap at more than 230 miles an hour, reaching the magic figure on the third day.

His lap of 230.432 at 11:44 a.m. May 4 was later exceeded by teammate Jim Crawford and Michael Andretti, but he broke the ground.

"I got a tow from (Scott) Pruett when I was still warming up at 226, but the others I was on my own," Guerrero said. "The chassis is working like a dream."

He was in the top three on every practice day leading up to pole qualifying. And he made history again

with a four-lap average of 232.482 miles an hour for a track record and his first "500' pole.

"I saw them on the dial and they looked pretty good," Guerrero said. "As soon as I went by the start/finish line, I ran out of fuel. Talk about close!" During the parade lap on Race Day, though, Guerrero suddenly broke to the left just off the second turn and hit the inside wall.

From his first pole position, he dropped to 33rd and out before the green flag waved.

"I hoped it was a dream or a nightmare," the popular veteran said sadly. "Obviously, with the cold weather, I was just trying to warm up the tires. I just gave it a little too much and it swapped ends."

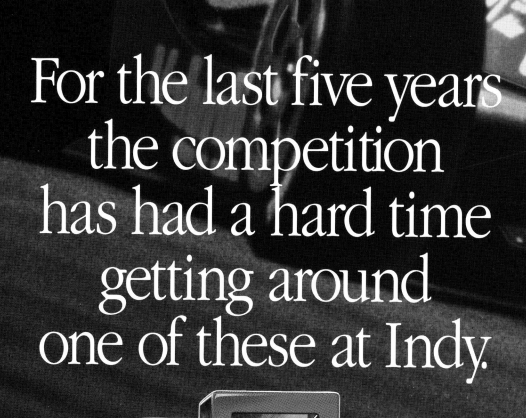

For the last five years the competition has had a hard time getting around one of these at Indy.

Congratulations, Al Unser Jr., Winner of the Indy 500.

Everyone talks about how racing technology makes their street cars better. What they fail to

say is whose technology has won more than anyone else. Chevrolet. The Heartbeat of America.™

For Those Who TRIED...

Not everyone who enters the Indianapolis 500 is guaranteed a start on race day, that honor being reserved for the fastest 33 qualifiers in four-lap time trials. There were 47 different drivers who competed during practice. We salute those who were not among the final 33.

Kenji Momota came within a whisker of becoming the second Japanese driver ever to qualify for an Indianapolis 500, but while his surprising final-day qualifying run of 218.967 mph did not hold up for a starting position, it missed by only a scant two-tenths of a mile per hour. He was the second alternate starter.

Three-time winner Johnny Rutherford made a valiant last-minute attempt at qualifying for what would have been his 25th "500" start. He was plagued by sponsorship problems, and by the time he managed to put together a program with Derrick Walker there was hardly any time left with which to build up to speed. His right-at-the-deadline run of 217.150 mph wasn't quite fast enough to earn a starting position.

Record books of the future will likely carry several asterisks next to the name of Mike Groff concerning his role in the 1992 "500." He was in the unusual position of earning a starting berth for a race in which he did not compete, while the car he qualified finished 2nd. What happened was this: Scott Goodyear had two Walker Motorsports cars at his disposal, but the car he preferred suffered an engine problem during practice on the first day of time trials. Rather than wait for a change of engine, Goodyear decided instead to qualify his "backup" car, but the speed he posted was slower than he would have liked. After spending the next week practicing his "prime" car at speeds which were considerably faster, he would gladly have substituted it for the qualified "backup" had such a move been permitted here. After considering several options, the Walker team hired Mike Groff to qualify the "prime" car on the understanding that Groff would switch cars with Goodyear for the race. Although driver substitutions have been made in other years, a "double-switch" of this type, while perfectly within rules, has never been executed before. Had it occurred, the cars would have been moved back to 32nd and 33rd for the start. As is turned out, Goodyear's speed did not hold up as one of the fastest 33 anyway, and he was "bumped" from the field just before qualifying concluded. A switch was made nevertheless, but it resulted in Goodyear starting last in the "prime" car while Groff watched from the sidelines. Groff might still have been included in the field in Goodyear's "bumped" car had any of the qualified cars been forced to withdraw before race day, but no such situation arose this year.

Tony Bettenhausen would just as soon as forget May of 1992. Failing to qualify for only the second time since his "rookie" start in 1981, he suffered through a contact with the wall plus three incomplete qualifying attempts.

There was a tragic end to Jovy Marcelo's attempt at becoming the first driver from the Philippines to drive in the "500." A tribute to this driver appears elsewhere in the Indy Review.

Belgian Didier Theys seemed virtually assured of a starting position once he signed on to drive John Andretti's Hall/VDS "backup," but nothing seemed to go right. After "waving off" two qualifying attempts at below the 220 at which he'd practiced, he blew an engine at the start of his third and final shot.

Hemelgarn-Byrd decided late in the month to run the Stan Fox "backup" with Pancho Carter driving. Pancho reached 223 in a hurry but handling problems dropped him down to 214 when he tried to qualify on day three. He hit the wall later the same day and a broken right arm halted any chance of making the race.

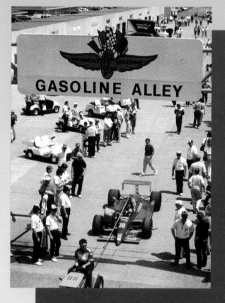

Italian Fabrizio Barbazza had the rather unusual distinction of placing third as a "rookie" in the 1987 "500," then never returning after that -- not even as a spectator. Until 1992, that is. He practiced at over 220 this year, but parted company with the Arciero team after his second wall contact in seven days. Johnny Parsons came on board for the final qualifying weekend, but was unable to earn a starting position.

It is amazing that Mark Dismore should have even visited the Speedway, let alone tried to qualify for the race following last year's horrendous accident and subsequent injuries during practice. Achieving only 216.7 mph after two weeks of concentrated effort with the Comet Kart Sales #66 this year, he jumped into a second Dave Mann entry on the final day and "almost" made it. He felt he could have improved upon his 218.4 with just a few more minutes of practice.

A tremendous amount of international interest was generated by the presence of renowned three-time World Champion Nelson Piquet of Brazil. Although coming from vastly differing backgrounds, he and teammate Gary Bettenhausen took to each other as brothers, the extraordinary rapport between them being quite obvious in this photograph. Sadly, Piquet crashed heavily during the first week of practice, sustaining serious injuries to his feet and ankles. That's public address announcer Tom Carnegie (right) sharing in their fun early in the month.

Japan's Hiro Matsushita worked up to 224 in preparation for what would have been his second "500," but he broke his leg in an accident during practice on the first day of qualifications. Raul Boesel drove Hiro's "backup" car in the race.

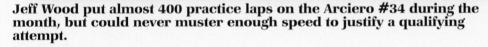

Jeff Wood put almost 400 practice laps on the Arciero #34 during the month, but could never muster enough speed to justify a qualifying attempt.

After leaving the Arciero team, Fabrizio Barbazza took a handful of laps in the Euromotorsports #42 prior to that team's decision not to attempt to qualify.

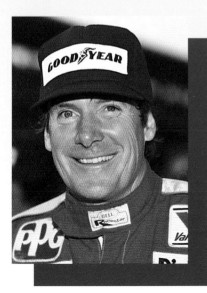

Large-framed Rocky Moran had to give up his assignment in one of the Menard cars because his body would not fit comfortably into the tight confines of the cockpit.

LOOK FOR RANDOMLY
PACKAGED AUTOGRAPHED
CARDS BY RICK MEARS

"*Legends of Indy*"™
RACING COLLECTOR CARDS

The **LEGENDS OF INDY** trading cards, which premiered in 1991, are back on track for 1992!
The **ALL NEW 1992** edition of 100 cards includes:
- **ALL 33 QUALIFYING DRIVERS FROM 1991** • **SPECIAL CELEBRITY CARDS**
- **PACE CARS OF THE '80s** • **1991 RACE ACTION PHOTOS**
- **GREAT HISTORY SHOTS**

LIMITED QUANTITIES AVAILABLE! Don't be left out of the race.
Get your cards today.

AVAILABLE AT:

BETTER CARD COLLECTORS' STORES, <u>TOYS R US</u>, AND
<u>THE INDIANAPOLIS 500 GIFT SHOP AND OFFICIAL SOUVENIR STANDS.</u>

DEVELOPED EXCLUSIVELY BY GRAND STAND SPORTS

1 (800)-866-0776

Walt Disney studios are very much in evidence with this huge stretch limo containing Mickey, Minnie, Roger Rabbit and Goofy.

BEFORE THE ROAR

Indianapolis Motor Speedway Chairman of the Board Mari Hulman George found the morning a little brisk.

Rodger Ward and Jim Rathmann take a lap of honor in their 1962 and 1960 winning mounts.

That's Parnelli Jones in the very car with which he won the 1963 Indy 500.

Troy Ruttman, the 1952 winner, cruises around with the "roadster" with which A.J. Foyt won his first 500 in 1961.

107

The starting field is "gridded," led by Roberto Guerrero's polesitter.

A flyover by a flight of Navy jets gets plenty of attention!

A.J. Foyt, preparing for his phenomenal record 35th consecutive Indy start, makes a last-minute adjustment.

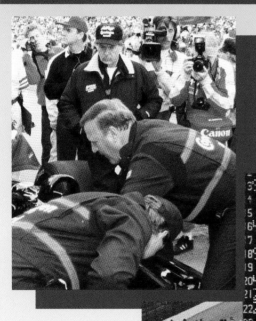

The 500 Festival Queen and her court return from a lap around the track.

I'm Free

Don't grieve for me, for now I'm free,
I'm following the path God laid for me,
I took his hand when I heard him call,
Into his kingdom my life will fall.

I could not stay another day,
To laugh, to love, to work or play,
Tasks left undone must stay that way,
I found that peace at the close of day.

If my parting has left a void,
Then fill it with remembering joy,
A friendship shared, a laugh, a kiss,.
Oh yes, these things I too will miss.

Be not burdened with times of sorrow,
My life's been full, I've savored much,
Good friends, good times, a loved ones touch.

Perhaps my time seemed all too brief,
Lift up your hearts and share with me,
God wanted me now, he set me free.

Indiana-born actress Florence Henderson gives her rendering of "America, The Beautiful."

elivers
l song
Again In
ousands

Sandi Patti sings the National Anthem.

Chairman of the Board Emeritus Mary Fendrich Hulman prepares to say, "Lady and gentlemen, start your engines!"

RACE TO THE BRICKS

by Gordon Kirby

"There is a God!" proclaimed the message scrawled across the windshield of Al Unser Jr's motorhome. An hour or so earlier Unser had finally won his first Indianapolis 500, passing beneath the checkered flag half a car length ahead of Scott Goodyear in the closest finish in the "500's" seventy-six year history. In his tenth try after a long, uncompetitive and unreliable month, Al Jr came from behind to score his own first victory and his family's eighth triumph in America's most famous motor race. He had finally carved his name in the pantheon of America's great drivers in company with his father Al and uncle Bobby.

Al Jr spent much of the 76th "500" fighting to stay unlapped. In fact he did lose a lap during the second round of pitstops, getting the lap back under the yellow some forty laps later. Nor had Unser been very competitive throughout the month, resorting to dramatic rear suspension changes on the eve of the race. A strong run through the second half of the race kept him in contention to win but until the eleventh hour "shoot-out" between Unser and Goodyear the race was dominated by Michael Andretti. Michael led all but twenty-nine laps before trickling to a stop with just eleven laps to go when the rubber drive belt at the front of his Ford engine broke.

From the start the race was entirely dominated by Andretti's Ford-Cosworth powered Newman-Haas Lola and the similar Ganassi Lola-Fords driven by Eddie Cheever and Arie Luyendyk. Michael and father Mario passed Cheever on either side in the first turn at the start so that the four Lola-Fords led the opening lap in the order - Michael, Mario, Luyendyk and Cheever.

There had been a lot of pre-race talk about the first turn, centering on some ill-feeling between Cheever and the senior Andretti following an incident in the previous month's Long Beach GP. But it came to nothing as Cheever backed off to allow the Andrettis to pass him on both sides. And right away the luckless Mario was immediately in trouble with a misfire, his terrible fortune at Indianapolis continuing its sorry story. At the first yellow he had to make for the

pits, losing three laps curing the problem which was caused by a crimped spark plug wire.

While the 1969 race winner's crew worked to solve the problem the three other Lola-Fords proceeded to set the pace chased only by Scott Brayton's Lola-Buick and Emerson Fittipaldi's Penske-Chevy. Such was Michael's pace that he was two, four, six and then eight seconds ahead after each of the opening four laps. However a rash of accidents and blown engines kept the field in closer order that might have been suggested by Michael's fierce pace.

The first of many incidents on an uncommonly cold, windy day came on the pace lap when poleman Roberto Guerrero spun and clipped the wall while trying to warm-up his tires. "I hoped it was a dream or a nightmare," explained the desolated Guerrero. "With the cold weather I was just trying to warm-up the tires. I just gave it a little too much and it swapped ends." So ended what until then had been the month's finest fairytale comeback story.

As far as incidents and accidents there was much more to come. Eleven laps into the race the first of seven serious accidents took place when Tom Sneva lost it and crashed heavily coming out of turn four. Sneva was lucky to escape with bruises to his feet, chest and hip. For a little while the race resumed without trouble, a 100-mile segment following Sneva's accident without a yellow. This enabled the flying Michael Andretti, running laps as quick as 226 mph, to lap everyone but Cheever and Fittipaldi. Then the race was seriously slowed and disrupted by accident after accident as the frigid north wind took all the heat out of the tires, causing more than a few drivers to lose control during the restarts. In these conditions new tires were as cool as the ambient temperature and with the wind chill factored-in it was less than forty degrees throughout the race!

The first of these rapid-fire crashes saw rookie Philippe Gache hit the wall. Gache in turn was hit hard by Stan Fox's car and both men were amazed to walk away from the wreckage without any injuries. Then on the restart Jim Crawford spun and crashed while trying to pass John Andretti. Crawford was collected by four-time winner Mears eliminating both on the spot. And right behind them '89 winner Fittipaldi lost it on his own, clouting the wall so that in one fell swoop Penske's two primary cars were written-off.

Crawford, Mears and Fittipaldi were taken to the hospital but were quickly released after treatment. Crawford escaped with a minor fracture of his left foot. Fittipaldi got away with some abrasions and a relatively insignificant leg wound. Mears banged his already well-battered feet and badly sprained his right wrist which required a brace

Top; Race morning temperatures caused fans to huddle. Bottom; Car owner Kenny Bernstein reacts to Roberto Guerrero's parade lap wreck.

Opposite; The field thunders into the first turn.

	Car	
Pos.	**No.**	**Driver**
1	1	Michael Andretti
2	9	Eddie Cheever
3	22	Scott Brayton
4	6	Arie Luyendyk
5	5	Emerson Fittipaldi
6	12	Bobby Rahal
7	51	G. Bettenhausen
8	26	Jim Crawford
9	8	John Andretti
10	3	Al Unser Jr.

100 MILES

Top; 1983 winner Tom Sneva was the first to make contact with the turn four wall on lap 11. Left; Starter Duane Sweeney displayed yellow 13 different times during the day. Bottom; Rookie Philippe Gache connected with the turn one wall on lap 66.

when driving for the next couple of months.

The next restart saw Mario Andretti crash heavily in the fourth turn, he too a victim of pushing too hard, too early in the bitterly cold conditions. He later said his mistake was in not burning-out his new rear tires as he left the pits under the yellow. "I didn't burn-out the tires because I was trying to save the gearbox and the engine and everything," said Andretti. "In retrospect that was a mistake because in burning-out the tires as you leave the pits it helps take the glaze off the tires and get them up to temperature."

Mario's car hit the wall head-on and he was taken to Methodist Hospital for four hours of surgery to broken toes, including both big toes. He was released three days later with a full cast on his left foot and was back racing three weeks later.

Andretti explained the accident: "On the restart I was accelerating gingerly, not running hard. I was just getting up to speed and there were four slower cars I could see in front of me. I just dived down to go underneath them and to my surprise it just went around. It really caught me by surprise."

Before the race was over other accidents claimed the cars driven by rookies Jimmy Vasser and Brian Bonner and by Jeff Andretti, Gary Bettenhausen and Arie Luyendyk. Bonner, Bettenhausen and Luyendyk were virtually uninjured but Vasser broke his right thigh bone and was out of action for three weeks.

Most grieviously injured driver on this black day was Mario's younger son Jeff Andretti who suffered serious injuries to both feet and legs after the right rear hub broke on his Foyt Lola-Chevrolet. Andretti spent the next two months in Methodist Hospital, undergoing a series of reconstruction operations. Like triple World Champion Nelson Piquet, injured badly during practice, Andretti says he wants to race again at Indianapolis.

Also eliminated when young Andretti crashed was veteran Gary Bettenhausen. One of the faster runners all month Bettenhausen started fifth but was lapped by flying Michael Andretti just after the first hundred miles. Hanging-in there in tenth place two laps down after 112 laps, Gary got involved in Jeff Andretti's accident, and hit the inside wall.

1990 winner Arie Luyendyk had looked a possible winner again in '92, running a strong second to Michael Andretti when he crashed in turn four on lap 136. Luyendyk was unable to match teammate Cheever's pace in the early laps of the race but after some pitside adjustments he ran quicker and quicker, soon overhauling Cheever and looking more and more like a potential winner. Running eight seconds behind Andretti on lap 136 however, he lost it while lapping four-time winner A.J. Foyt. The Texas veteran had been running without a leftside mirror, its lens knocked-out by debris from the many incidents, and A.J. didn't see Arie going underneath him.

Top; Jim Crawford spun in turn two and collected four-time winner Rick Mears. Right; Car owner Paul Newman awaits word on Mario Andretti who spun in turn four. Bottom; Emerson Fittipaldi crashed attempting to slow down for the Crawford-Mears accident.

"We made some changes and the car got better and better," reported Luyendyk. "The car felt good and I went underneath Foyt going into turn four. He pinched me down to the apron and I hit the bump between the track and the apron. That got both front wheels bouncing into the air so that I had no steering. I was lucky I was able to get it turned a little bit before the wall so I hit sideways. Fortunately it wasn't too bad."

Top; Michael Andretti under Ford power was clearly the man to catch. Bottom; Michael passed Arie Luyendyk who had developed handling problems.

These various incidents decimated the field and reduced the pace of the race so that it was the slowest Indy 500 since 1958. Nevertheless Michael Andretti continued to set a scorching pace under the green, running laps as fast as 229 mph! With Cheever being penalized one lap for passing some lapped cars under the yellow, Andretti was left alone to fly the Ford flag chased by an impressive Scott Goodyear and Al Unser Jr, each with Chevrolet power, and four-time winner Al Unser with a Buick engine. Going into the final seventy miles the race was between these four with Michael looking more and more unbeatable.

Pos.	Car No.	Driver
	200 MILES	
1	1	Michael Andretti
2	9	Eddie Cheever
3	6	Arie Luyendyk
4	12	Bobby Rahal
5	3	Al Unser Jr.
6	22	Scott Brayton
7	15	Scott Goodyear
8	7	Paul Tracy
9	27	Al Unser
10	18	Danny Sullivan

A little earlier Al Sr became possibly the only driver to pass Michael during the 76th "500." At the time Michael had stopped for fuel and tires under a yellow and was running directly ahead of Unser for the restart. Unser was at the other end of his fuel load with worn tires and four laps after the restart he dived inside Andretti only to be repassed on the following lap. "I was pretty surprised when

Snap-on. The Difference Between Winning And Just Racing.

Rick Mears is a guy who knows a few things about finishing first. He's one of the premier drivers in CART racing. In fact, he was the driver of the decade with more victories in the 80's than any other Indy car driver.

But as good as he is, as competitive as he is, Rick Mears doesn't take any unnecessary chances.

Neither does his team. The Penske Racing Team is unquestionably the best in the business. The best prepared. And the best equipped. It's no coincidence that they're the most successful team in CART history. No one can match the Penske Team's 63 wins or their seven first place finishes at Indy.

Their tools? Snap-on. The Penske Team won't settle for anything less. Because they know Snap-on subscribes to the same high standards of quality and performance.

Snap-on tools are designed better and built better. They fit precisely. They deliver superior torque. They're balanced with just the right feel in your hand. And they're made to last.

Are Rick Mears and the Penske Team obsessed? You bet. With being number one. And you don't go after number one with anything but the number one tools. Snap-on.

Snap-on Tools Corporation, Kenosha, WI 53141-1410

OFFICIAL TOOLS OF

CAM

CHAMPIONSHIP
ASSOCIATION OF
MECHANICS, INC.

he passed me," Michael later commented. "I actually thought at that point Al was the fastest car out there."

The final round of pitstops took place with just over twenty laps or fifty miles to go. Back on the track Andretti led Eddie Cheever by eight seconds and Goodyear by only twenty-two seconds with Unser barely a second behind in third place and his father Al Sr continuing to run well in fourth despite a slow final pitstop which dropped him out of contact with Goodyear and his son. With a dozen laps to go Al Jr passed Goodyear in traffic for second place and on the following lap the fabled Andretti-Indianapolis bad luck struck poor Michael who suddenly coasted to a stop on the track, his engine's fuel pump drive belt broken after a superb demonstration. A desolate Michael immediately left the track, going to Methodist Hospital to visit his injured father and brother.

Above; Scott Brayton's strong run was stopped by a blown engine. Bottom; Michael Andretti used quick service in the pits to maintain his lead.

300 MILES		
Pos.	Car No.	Driver
1	1	Michael Andretti
2	6	Arie Luyendyk
3	9	Eddie Cheever
4	3	Al Unser Jr.
5	27	Al Unser.
6	15	Scott Goodyear
7	12	Bobby Rahal
8	18	Danny Sullivan
9	11	Raul Boesel
10	14	A.J. Foyt Jr.

"It can't get much worse than this," commented Michael. "This place is cruel, so cruel. It was really hard to keep my concentration. First dad and then Jeff. I knew Jeff's was bad. I knew I still had a job to do but it was hard to concentrate. I thought I was getting the job done. The car was perfect. I've never had a car so perfect. It looks like a fuel pump put us out but we're not sure yet. Man, after seeing what happened to dad and Jeff, this is really hard to take."

The following day Michael described his unhappy 76th "500." "A couple of times we gave up the lead to make pitstops just to change tires," explained

THE BEST WAY TO DO LAPS AT THE INDY 500.

Enjoy the Great American
Sundae Cone during the Greatest
Spectacle in Racing.® And it won't even
take you 200 laps to finish.

Nestlé.

Andretti. "With so many accidents there was debris and carbon fiber chips blowing around. The carbon chips are just impossible to find and clean up. USAC and the safety crews did a great job but the conditions made things very dangerous. You had to be careful and use your head. That's why we came in for new tires a few times, to be sure that we hadn't picked anything up in the tires we'd been running a the time of the accident."

"My plan," he went on, "since I had a pretty dominant race car was to get out front and try to lap as many people as possible. If we had fifty to sixty laps of green I think I would have been able to lap the field. As the race went on I became more and more confident. The car was just perfect and we ran in sixth gear - a real, long overdrive - all the way."

As well as setting the race's fastest lap at more than 229 mph on lap 166, Michael's dominance was such that he recorded all eleven fastest laps of the 76th "500" and no fewer than 22 of the race's fastest 25 laps! He did so despite knowing that his father and brother were injured after driving past their wrecked cars and hearing reports on their conditions over his radio. "Trying to keep your concentration was very, very tough," admitted Andretti the day after the race. "That's the downside of having relations in racing. But more than ever, this tells me that family is everything in life."

The yellow flag came out to remove Michael's stalled car. Then the green flag waved with seven laps to go. Unser and Goodyear raced nose to tail to the checkered flag with Goodyear trying all he knew to find a way around Unser. Goodyear was quicker in the third and fourth turns but Unser had the legs of

the Canadian in the first and second turns. Unser weaved down the straights to keep Goodyear behind him and then had to lift for a moment when his car slid in the fourth turn on the 200th and final lap.

"I ran wide-open from the yellow flag," reported Unser. "I never lifted until turn four on the last lap when I had to breathe it a little because my car was a little loose. When I had to do that I looked in my mirrors and Scott was right under my exhaust. He was all in my mirrors and I tried to make the race car as wide as I could. I was talking to my Chevy and to my Galmer saying, 'Come on. 'Let's go!'"

Commented Goodyear: "I don't know if I'd call it blocking. I'd call it using the race track and I would have done the same thing. On the second last lap I got some bad air from Al's car and had to get out of

400 MILES		
Pos.	Car No.	Driver
1	1	Michael Andretti
2	15	Scott Goodyear
3	3	Al Unser Jr.
4	27	Al Unser
5	9	Eddie Cheever
6	18	Danny Sullivan
7	12	Bobby Rahal
8	11	Raul Boesel
9	14	A.J. Foyt Jr.
10	93	John Paul Jr.

DieHard. How the legends get their start.

Most legendary Indy drivers know the battery with the power to start their cars is exactly the same as the battery you can buy for your car. DieHard. The battery that has been starting more than 75 million Americans over the past 25 years.

You can count on Sears DieHard® batteries to consistently deliver more power when you need it most. After all, who backs you better than Sears?

'You Can Count on me.'
SEARS

Al Unser Jr. was quite aware that his father was closing in from the third postion.

the throttle. Then on the last lap I started catching him in turns three and four and started to get a good tow. He knew it and he weaved."

On the run down to the checkered flag Goodyear pulled beside Unser, both cars moving close to the pit wall. Unser was half a car length in front at the flag, winning by 0.043 seconds to record the closest finish in the history of the Indianapolis 500, closer even than the famous finish between Johncock and Mears in 1982.

"With five laps to go," commented Goodyear, "I was flat in sixth gear and I knew we had too much drag in the car. I'd been passed by Al when we came up on a lapped car and his car seemed a little freer and quicker in traffic than mine. At the finish I knew it was going to be very close. I just hoped the finish line was another hundred yards down the road."

Said Unser: "I was looking for the white flags on the 198th lap and they weren't there. We went around again and I started to think about the infamous last lap. I couldn't take my mind off Scott. He was doing a heck of a job and his car was working well. I started to get a little emotional but I had to concentrate on what I had to do. Scott definitely kept me honest and almost took it away from me coming down the front straightaway on the last lap."

Unser's first victory at Indianapolis came after a long, hard month wherein he blew five engines in practice and fought with a loose or tail-happy car most of

IF VALVOLINE DIDN'T PERFORM, NEITHER WOULD AL UNSER JR.

Valvoline, Inc. A Subsidiary of Ashland Oil, Inc. ⊕ ·Lexington, KY 40509 © 1991

You don't get to be the 1990 PPG Indy Car World Series Champion and a regular on the leader board by just being a good driver. It requires greatness–in your car and motor oil too. That's why it should come as no surprise that Al Unser, Jr. chooses to use Valvoline in his race car—and his own car. In fact, Valvoline is the number one choice of Indy 500 chief mechanics for use in their race cars and their *own* cars. Which is all the more reason to let Valvoline perform for you too. PEOPLE WHO KNOW USE VALVOLINE®

"It's every bit a good feeling as I thought it was going to be plus more." -- Al Unser Jr.

the time. He was well off the pace on "Carburetion Day" and the Galles-Kraco team made some dramatic changes to Unser's Galmer for the race, installing a new rear suspension set-up which the team had not tested at Indianapolis.

"To be real honest with you," said Unser, "we still haven't got the mechanical part of our car figured out. One of my saviors today was the fact that it was so cool. It might have been a different story if the weather had been hot and the track was slippery. But the car worked beautifully all day. The front end was sticking and the back end was sticking pretty good as well."

Al Jr's teammate Danny Sullivan finished a lap down in fifth place so that team owner Rick Galles was a very happy man that night. "We were on the pole in Australia with Al Jr and then won Long Beach with Danny. Now we've won Indianapolis so I think this shows our detractors that we've got a little bit of potential. We took a gamble on building our own car and our designer Alan Mertens has his whole life in this project. It's been tough to get it going but I think now you're seeing the results of everyone's

500 MILES

Pos.	Car No.	Driver
1	3	Al Unser Jr.
2	15	Scott Goodyear
3	27	Al Unser
4	9	Eddie Cheever
5	18	Danny Sullivan
6	12	Bobby Rahal
7	11	Raul Boesel
8	8	John Andretti
9	14	A.J. Foyt Jr.
10	93	John Paul Jr.

YOU DON'T GO BACK TO BASICS. YOU TAKE THEM FORWARD.

There is a curious shift in business these days, "back to the basics." And it seems as if the sophisticated fast-trackers of the '80s have been transformed into the business fundamentalists of the '90s.

Nice try, guys. The simple truth is, basics are something you start with and take forward. Not retreat to.

In the past 10 years we've become a $12 billion insurance company by embracing the ageless basics of common sense and simplicity and bringing them into a new age of technology and management.

This has allowed us to centralize and streamline operations in ways never possible before. Allowed us to create products that are profitable against today's ever-changing financial landscape. Allowed us to establish the most cost-effective means of distribution. And, allowed us to be more active managers of our investment portfolio.

The basics. By taking them forward, they've taken us forward. To where we are today, to where we'll be tomorrow.

© 1992 Conseco, Inc.

Conseco

Scott Goodyear made his third Indy start a memorable one coming from 33rd to finish just a tick behind Al Unser Jr.

efforts in this team."

Mertens was in seventh heaven after the race. "This is a fairy tale ending to a really hard month," said Mertens. "We gambled on the new rear suspension and at the end of the race we gambled on putting unscrubbed sticker tires on the car. I think the tires helped Al catch Goodyear but then at the end the performance of the tires fell off and it was all in Junior's hands.

"Track conditions did suit us today," Mertens went on. "I was delighted yesterday when I saw it was going to be cool. That definitely helped us. I have to say Junior has been unbelievably patient all month. He hasn't got uptight through all the problems we've had. He just kept at it. He deserves to win it."

For his part Unser was delighted to finally join his father and uncle as an Indy 500 winner. The family now boasts no fewer than eight victories at Indianapolis, dating back to uncle Bobby's first win in 1968.

"It's every bit as good a feeling as I thought it was going to be plus more, " grinned Al Jr. "Riding the pace car around the track on the victory lap was just awesome. In the fourth turn Rick (Galles) said, 'Pinch me and tell me this is really happening and it's not just a dream!' Then we saw dad and we hugged each other. There were tears in both of our eyes."

Runnerup Goodyear's performance was his best yet and opened everyone's eyes to his ability. By coming from 33rd and last in the field to finish second the 32-year old Canadian also equalled Tom Sneva's record-setting performance from a dozen years ago. Excellent pit strategy by Goodyear's Walker Motorsports team helped him on his way. The team also worked hard during the month to solve an engine oiling problem, going through five engines and three different oil tanks before finding a race day solution to the problem.

"I think the most important thing today was two-fold," commented Goodyear. "The first thing was staying out of trouble and the second thing which was very important was to make sure the tires were warm enough before you really leaned on the car. We all saw the accidents and knew you had to be careful. I had one incident on a restart where I had the car really step-out on me in turn four. It really did a tank-slapper but I was fortunate to catch it and carry on."

Also running the full, 200 laps was four-time winner Al Unser. Starting 22nd after replacing the injured Nelson Piquet in one of John Menard's Lola-Buicks, Unser drove a typically clean, unspectacular race. Five days before his 53rd birthday Unser avoided all the wrecks and finished a strong third in his first Indy car race in more than a year. Big Al's fine effort was the best result ever for Buick at Indianapolis as well as the fifth time in the last ten years that he's finished the Indy 500 in the top three.

Rookie Lyn St. James, only the second woman to start at Indy, finished 11th and collected Rookie of the Year honors.

Fresh,

Pure &

Natural.

The Only

Beer

With The

Genuine

Taste Of

The King

Of

Beers.

©1992 ANHEUSER-BUSCH, INC. •BUDWEISER® •ST. LOUIS, MO

"This is a very proud and happy day for me," commented the senior Unser. "To see my boy finally win this race makes me very proud and I'm happy for myself to come through a race like this and give the guys in John Menard's team a good day because they really needed it. I'm happy for them."

Fourth place went to Eddie Cheever who was originally awarded sixth place with a lap penalty for passing under the yellow. A review of scoring by USAC resulted in the penalty being rescinded however so that the following day's official results had Cheever in fourth, the last car to complete all 200 laps. A lap behind in fifth and sixth places were Al Jr's teammate Sullivan and '86 winner Bobby Rahal. A flat tire midway through the race lost Rahal a lap and cost him a shot at winning the 76th "500."

"My car was great," commented Rahal. "I ran over some debris in the middle of the race and cut a tire. It almost got away from me in turn four when that happened. Then I almost hit the fence as I was trying to get to the pits because the car was sitting down on the right rear corner. But I have to say I feel like I won today just to be able to walk out of here after this race with myself and the car in one piece."

Seventh place was taken by Raul Boesel. Two laps down at the finish Boesel drove a solid race for Dick Simon's team in place of the injured Hiro Matsushita. After sitting-out the previous year Boesel earned himself a regular ride with Simon with his good run at Indianapolis. "The hardest part of the race was to keep concentration and not let down because of all the long yellows," said Boesel. "The car ran like a clock all day. No problems whatsoever. It was a really fine race for me."

Finishing three laps behind Boesel in eighth place was John Andretti. Coming in a little too hot for his first pitstop, John brushed the wall in his pit and knocked two of his crewmen to the ground. The incident bent a front wing and steering arm and more time was lost in trying to repair the damage. "I can't believe I did that," uttered Andretti about the incident which cost him a chance of finishing higher. "It was my fault completely. I just messed up."

Four-time winner Foyt finished on the same lap as Andretti in ninth place. His race was solid but unspectacular and at the following evening's victory banquet he was uncommonly reserved. "That wasn't the same A.J. Foyt you saw out there this year," he quietly declared.

Tenth place went to John Paul Jr who struggled all day with a misfire. Completing the finishers in eleventh and twelfth places were Lyn St. James and Dominic Dobson, both whom ran 193 of the 200 laps. St. James was only the second woman ever to start the "500" and the following night she was proclaimed the race's Rookie of the Year, the realization for St. James of a long-held dream.

Gordon Kirby is North American editor of the English weekly magazine 'Autosport' and Editor at Large of the monthly 'Racer'.

Tanner

My Hero, My Friend JIMMY BRYAN

Len Gasper
Phil Sampaio

Gasper
Sampaio

My Hero, My Friend JIMMY BRYAN

Len Gasper, Phil Sampaio

"Len Gasper has been a loyal friend for several years. I've found that he is not only the type of person who admires the skill required to become a top driver but also sees us in the light of the individuals that we really are. No one could give you more insight into Jimmy Bryan the driver and the man than Len in his book, *My Hero, My Friend.*"

Arie Luyendyk
1990 Indianapolis 500 Winner

"Most people would remember Jimmy Bryan in the shiny white racer barking the throttle of an Offenhauser engine and the smell of racing fuels as he broadslid through the mile ovals throughout the United States. But there was a lot more to that man than just racing. There was a personal, quiet side to him. Jimmy let me know on a personal level that I should never be afraid to dream. With my involvement in motor sports today, I only wish I could thank him. Now, the Jimmy Bryan I knew and loved as a boy, returns in *My Hero, My Friend.*"

Army Armstrong
TNN and ESPN
Motorsports Commentator

"For those of us whoever had a childhood idol, *My Hero, My Friend* is a must reading. The compelling story between Len Gasper and his legendary hero, Jimmy Bryan, will warm even the coldest hearts. It is a treasure to be enjoyed not only by race fans, but by everyone who has ever dared to dream."

John E. Blazier
Founder and President,
National Indy 500
Collector's Club

Ralph Tanner Associates, Inc.
Book Publishers
122 North Cortez Street, Suite 102
Prescott, Arizona 86301

My Hero, My Friend JIMMY BRYAN

Len Gasper
Phil Sampaio

Introduction by Sam Hanks

My Hero, My Friend is the story of two people. A boy named Len Gasper and his hero, Jimmy Bryan. The story takes place during the 1950s and recounts the events of that era. Throughout the story, the life and racing accomplishments of Jimmy Bryan are told, as well as the close friendship that developed between Gasper and Bryan.

My Hero, My Friend takes an intimate look into the life of a legendary racing figure and shows the elements of personality that made Jimmy Bryan, the "Arizona Cowboy" - loved by millions. *My Hero, My Friend* also chronicles the history of Champ Car/Indy Car racing during the 1950s, and the pioneers of the sport. Among several of the great drivers mentioned in the story are Bill Vukovich, Jack McGrath, Bob Sweikert, Pat Flaherty, Sam Hanks, Pat O'Connor, Johnny Boyd, Tony Bettenhausen, Jim Rathmann, and Troy Ruttman.

Unlike the stereotypical stories of old, dealing with reckless hell-raising race car drivers, *My Hero, My Friend* is an impassioned piece of work that addresses the human side of racing. Written by Phil Sampaio, as told by Len Gasper, the story is a fascinating, personal look into the world of racing and a wonderful and unforgettable man named Jimmy Bryan, whose memory will live on through the pages of this book.

Deluxe Hardcover Edition. A limited edition book with six-color dust jacket. This book is an impressive 7" x 10" format, and features state-of-the art graphics and printing. The 326 pages include 62 rare and exciting photographs. The cost is $35.00, plus $3.50 for UPS delivery. Arizona residents please add $2.35 for sales tax. (U.S. Dollars).

Library of Congress: 92-081429
ISBN: 0-942078-19-5
Copyright ©1992 Len Gasper/Phil Sampaio

A Collector's Edition. Limited to 1,000 numbered and autographed copies, this edition features a gold-foil embossed cover. Also included is a deluxe embossed slip case. The six-color dust jacket, suitable for framing, is mailed in a separate container. The cost is $75.00, plus $3.50 for UPS delivery. Arizona residents please add $5.03 for sales tax. (U.S. Dollars). No Collector's Editions books reserved without payment.

Library of Congress: 92-081430
ISBN: 0-942078-20-9
Copyright ©1992 Len Gasper
Phil Sampaio

"My Hero, My Friend Jimmy Bryan" is available from your local bookstore; or order directly from Ralph Tanner Associates, Inc., Suite 102, 122 North Cortez Street, Prescott, AZ 86301. (Telephone 1-800-272-3692).

GREAT YEAR FOR GOODYEAR

by Gordon Kirby

As last year's race focused on a classic, two-man 'shoot-out' over the last ten laps, most of the huge crowd, not to mention radio and television audiences, had no idea who the fellow was in the blue and silver car running hard on Al Unser Jr.'s tail. It was of course, Scott Goodyear, a 32-year old Canadian who was competing in his third Indianapolis 500. He finished tenth, nine laps behind in 1990, his rookie year. In '91 Goodyear's Judd engine blew up early in the proceedings. And after starting the 76th "500" from the last row after blowing-up five engines during the two weeks of practice, there was Goodyear trying to chase down Al Jr. and put his face on the Borg-Warner Trophy.

With his name suddenly in the limelight Goodyear tried mighty hard to beat Unser and when Al Jr. got sideways in turn four on the last lap, the unknown Canadian suddenly had a chance to pull-off the impossible. As Unser got back on the throttle and pulled his car under control Goodyear started steaming down the inside with enough momentum maybe to catch Unser at the checkered flag. Al Jr. made Goodyear work for it, squeezing him a little, pushing Goodyear toward the pit wall and indeed it was all just a little too late, half a car length behind at the finish line.

"I knew it was going to be close," Goodyear sadly shook his head. "I just hoped it was another hundred yards down the road." Nevertheless, the finish was the closest in the "500's" history and it was Goodyear's best finish by far in three Indy 500s and forty-six Indy car starts. Suddenly he was known around the world and a national hero in Canada.

"I remember hearing Bobby Rahal say that winning Indy changed his life," remarked Goodyear. "Well as a Canadian, finishing second at Indy

Scott Goodyear advanced from 33rd starting position to challenge Al Jr. for the victory.

WORLD LEADER
IN AUTOMOTIVE
ELECTRONICS...

this year changed my life. In fact it's been overwhelming. There have been so many requests for interviews and appearances. It made things very busy and hectic but I can only say I'm very pleased. It's raised the awareness of our program and of racing in general in Canada to a whole new level."

Goodyear began racing more than twenty years ago, first in go-karts. He won many races and some championships in karts and started racing Formula Fords in Canada when he was twenty. The son of a motorcycle, snowmobile and go-kart dealer, Goodyear quickly showed he had the makings of a champion driver. He won three Canadian Formula Ford titles in a row, tried to race Formula 3 in Europe with very little money and came back from a financially-enforced year's layoff to win the 1986 Formula Atlantic championship.

In 1987 he ran his first Indy car race, driving for Dick Hammond's small team in a handful of road races. The following year he won Canada's Porsche Cup championship, then drove for Audi's factory GT team in Europe before finally getting the Indy car break he was looking for with Jim O'Donnell's Mackenzie Financial team. O'Donnell was becoming disenchanted with driver Ludwig Heimrath Jr and in the summer of 1989 he decided to run a second car for Goodyear in the Toronto street race. Goodyear responded by racing up to ninth place before he was stopped by mechanical failure. That winter O'Donnell decided to sign Goodyear for his first full-time Indy car season.

Powered by Judd engines in 1990 and '91, Goodyear made his mark but didn't have the horsepower to run with the leaders. He qualified at Indianapolis both years and had his best race in the streets of Vancouver where he finished seventh. For the '92 season sponsor O'Donnell moved to Derrick Walker's team and right away things began to happen. With Chevrolet engines for the first time Goodyear finished fifth in April's Long Beach GP street race and ran fast before crashing on the one-mile Phoenix oval. When practice began at Indianapolis Goodyear again looked good, quickly running over 220 mph.

"When I first ran at Indianapolis in 1990," Goodyear began the story, "I thought I was just there to be in a ride and to try and stay out of trouble and stay out of people's way. In 1991 I felt like I knew a lot more and got the car set-up better so I could drive around flat-out quite easily with the Judd engine. I went there knowing we didn't have the power and that we probably wouldn't

Team owner Derrick Walker found a winning combination with Goodyear in the driver's seat.

finish the race because we never had gone over 300 miles with the Judd. But I could run flat-out even with full tanks in the race until we broke the motor on lap 37."

"This year," he went on, "I went to Indianapolis expecting a lot. I went there calculating in my mind what I wanted out of the deal. The first couple of days went well. We saw 224 mph and then we got into the oil system problems."

Goodyear started blowing engines and the team scrambled to find a solution to the problem. Team boss Walker decided to put Goodyear into the team's reliable, one-year old spare car for the first qualifying weekend and Scott duly put the car into the field while the team continued working on the problems with the '92 car. On the second weekend Walker put Mike Groff into the team's new car and when Goodyear's first weekend speed in the older car wasn't good enough to keep him in the field, Scott moved into helpmate Groff 's seat for the race, moving to 33rd and last starting position.

"When we qualified the '92 car with Mike Groff," commented Walker, "I was very concerned that the engine was going to blow up. We tried to do as few laps as possible to let him get up to speed because we knew the engine would not last." For the ride-less Groff it was a great opportunity to show his stuff in a tough situation even if it meant missing the race.

By the week of the race Walker's team finally had the oiling problems licked and on Carburetion Day Goodyear ran encouragingly well. "Because of all the problems we had never run very much on full tanks," commented Goodyear. "So on Carburetion Day we went out there on full tanks. We started off at forty gallons and ran it down to twenty-two gallons and filled it back up again. And all that time we were still running sixth or seventh quickest. When we came off the track I think we were ninth quickest and ended the day twelfth quickest.

"At the end of that day," he went on, "I thought we were going to be in good

Opposite; Derrick Walker and Goodyear coached Groff as he shook down the team's primary car.

Top; Mike Groff qualified for a race in which he did not compete. Bottom; Goodyear and Groff took a break during practice to discuss strategy.

143

shape for the race. The car was comfortable on full tanks and I could run anywhere I wanted to. So after a long, tiring month I was actually looking forward to the race. I went into that race thinking I've got nothing to lose as long as I can get through everything and be there at the end."

From the start Goodyear began moving through the field, making it to twentieth by the time of the first yellow after just eight laps! He continued to move up and then by deciding not to pit during the next yellow found himself in seventh place by lap twenty. Pitting under the green after thirty-seven laps Goodyear lost a lap to race leader Michael Andretti but he continued to run a strong pace.

"I was pretty upset when I got a lap down," commented Goodyear. "Then after a little while I was so pleased when Michael was behind the pace car and then myself and just a couple of laps before the pace car pulled off Michael ducked into the pits. That made me the first car behind the pace car and I thought if I could go out and pull away from these guys maybe I can get my lap back.

"We were able to run 220-221 mph laps and I actually pulled away from Al Sr," he continued. "I saw him in my mirror and he was creeping up on me ever so slightly. I was flat-out all the way around on full tanks, that was it. And he's catching up a little bit and then the yellow came. I got on the radio and told Derrick, Yellow! Yellow! Usually he tells me before I can tell him that there's a yellow but I saw it and I knew we had got the lap back.

"When that happened," Goodyear went on, "I thought well maybe there might be a chance today to run up there, to be there at the end. And when I realized we were really going to be there for a top three finish I was really happy. For me the rest of the race was just tremendous. I tried as hard as I could. The car worked really well. I don't think it was as quick as Al's car in traffic but it was really very good in clean air. When Al got sideways in the last turn on the last lap I thought we still had a chance but as it was we came a little short.

"At that moment it was very disappointing but then I started to realize that I'd finished second at the Indianapolis 500 and it felt pretty good. Then when I came down the pit lane and saw the guys in the team leaping up and down and saw the happiness in their faces, that was when I really started feeling good."

Goodyear is another of the modern breed of open-wheel road racers who has adapted well to oval tracks. He had virtually no oval racing experience before climbing into an Indy car but like some others he's shown he can very definitely do the job.

"I think I enjoy oval racing more than road racing because it's all about refinement," noted Goodyear. "The road courses are up and down, pounding in there and I love that because it's me inside. But it's different on the ovals, it's such a challenge to sit there and work on a guy - run him high, run him low, work on him, start to see his traits and his lines. Then all of a sudden bang! You've got him. That's fun!

"You have to be able to maneuver the car on an oval, to be able to run high and low," he went on. "The car can't operate as if it's on a one-track mind like it might in qualifying. Races on ovals are close quarters. It's challenging with everybody jockeying for position.

"I learned a lot even this past year at Indy running in traffic," concluded Goodyear. "I saw enough of the stuff! And you learn that if the car's not working on an oval, you can't be a hero. That's how I got into trouble at Phoenix. You just can't throw it in there and say OK, I'm gonna ride this thing because it's gonna ride you. I've learned that your butt doesn't lie to you on an oval. And I've learned that you have to understand more of what you want from the car on an oval."

Team owner Walker rates Goodyear very high. "Scott reminds me a little of Rick Mears," said Walker who worked with Mears during a long tenure with Penske Racing. "He's got a very clear, precise description of how the car reacts and defining what the problems may be. He has a good feel for the car and can get to the bottom of problems quicker than some guys might."

Goodyear's performance in the 76th Indy 500 gave Walker even more confi-

Goodyear easily made up the lap he lost when he pitted under green after 37 laps.

dence in his driver. "Through all kinds of conditions and plenty of restarts he was there all the time just plugging along, cool as a cucumber," commented Walker. "It was just, you know, 10-4 on the radio and he just kept going. Being there at the end is one of Scott's big pluses. He's a strong, sturdy little Canadian. He's like a dog fighter but very mild in manner. He's very much a thinking driver. The wheels are always turning."

Scott's wife Leslie bore the Goodyears their first child last February. Three months later Goodyear finished a fighting second at Indianapolis and on Canada's 125th birthday - July 1st - he was among a select group of Canadian sportsmen invited to meet England's Queen Elizabeth. A lot happened to Scott Goodyear in 1992 and he's hoping for more of the same, maybe better with Derrick Walker's team and Mackenzie sponsorship in '93. One place better at Indianapolis would do nicely.

Gordon Kirby is North American editor of the English weekly 'Autosport' and Editor at Large of 'Racer' magazine.

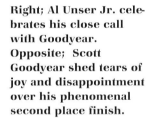

Right; Al Unser Jr. celebrates his close call with Goodyear. Opposite; Scott Goodyear shed tears of joy and disappointment over his phenomenal second place finish.

INDY REVIEW
CONTINUE THE COLLECTION

Now, Indy 500 Publications offers the annual *INDY REVIEW*, a collectible, hardbound book which chronicles the events and drama of the greatest automobile race in the world. Every edition is handsomely embossed and foil-stamped for your bookcase collection.

FEATURES:

- A review of the Indianapolis 500
- Full-color action photographs
- Features on teams, drivers and personalities

- In depth day-by-day narratives of the "Month of May", along with thorough statistical summaries.

ORDER THE PREMIER ISSUE
OF THE 1991 *INDY REVIEW*
(Add $4.95 for shipping and handling
plus state sales tax where applicable).

$24.95

ORDER NOW! CALL **1-800-955-INDY** TOLL FREE
9:00 a.m.-5:00 p.m. (EST)

Or write to: *Indy Review* • P.O. Box 24152 • Speedway, IN 46224

AFTER THE ROAR

by Jan Shaffer

There are several moments of universal emotion during the month of May at Indianapolis.

The first comes with Pole Day qualifying, as drivers and teams build up to speed to vie for front-row starting spots. The next comes when "bumping" starts, as those with frustrations try to insure a position in the 33-car lineup.

Pressures then mount toward Race Day, and a month — indeed, a year — of building, testing and planning come head-to-head with the payoff.

When that day is over, the PPG Indy Car World Series continues at race tracks throughout the land, but its focal point at Indy is history for another year.

Garages are cleaned out at the Speedway, transporters are loaded, and the lessons of one May turn into the strategy, innovation and technology of the next.

The days that follow are of reflection and relief, triumph and frustration, elation and reassessment.

For Al Unser, Jr., as with past "500" winners, came the endless string of personal appearances, television shows, interviews and the like, a duty for every Indy champion.

It may have started during post-race television interviews, when his happy wife, Shelley, turned to a friend and asked, "It's Sunday, and I want to get him a Western-style tux for the Victory Dinner. Do you know any place?"

Unser, Jr.'s margin of victory of .043 of a second over Scott Goodyear was the closest in "500" history, one of many milestones during the month of

Nelson Piquet, recovering from his injuries, hopes to return to Indy in 1993.

149

May. The drama of the finish was replayed over and over for television audiences around the world in a commercial for Valvoline, Unser, Jr.'s sponsor.

The Indianapolis 500 had been run on May 24 only three times in history, and an Unser had won it each time — Bobby in 1981, Al in 1987 and now Al Jr., in 1992.

It was a first "500" victory for Galles-Kraco Racing, or its previously separate race teams, and the Galmer chassis, a newcomer to the trail. For Chevrolet, it was a fifth straight victory at Indy.

For Scott Goodyear and Walker Motorsports, it was the best finish for a second-year team trying to go to the top of the Indy car world on a limited budget, a Cinderella story. The performance stayed with car owner Derrick Walker and Goodyear as a launching pad for things to come.

The race was also a triumph of sorts for the so-called "old guard," as Al Unser jumped into a Team Menard car to replace the injured Nelson Piquet and the four-time winner proved he still had the "right stuff" with a third-place finish. As with his fourth win in 1987, he is always a threat.

Others proved their mettle. Raul Boesel finished seventh, with minimal practice time in a Dick Simon Racing entry. John Paul, Jr., chugged to 10th in what may be Dave Mann's final Speedway entry as a car owner. Lyn St. James steadied to 11th en route to history in her first-ever Indy car race, with plans to return and improve on it.

But there are also those who didn't achieve their goals at Indianapolis, as there will always be.

The so-called "Andretti luck" provided the nightmares of both injury and loss to one of racing's first families. Michael had dominated the event, only to bow out with mechanical woes.

Mario Andretti's crash left him with broken toes, and caused him to miss a race because of injury for only the second time in his career. But after Teo Fabi subbed for him at Detroit, Mario was back in the saddle.

For Jeff Andretti, the recovery was to take longer. His accident left him with broken bones in both legs, feet and ankles, and he faced months of therapy and treatment. It would be a longer road back.

The same would be true for Nelson Piquet, the Formula One driver who had captured the hearts and attention of many around the Speedway.

When he had joined Team Menard as a teammate to Gary Bettenhausen, rail-birds dubbed them the "Odd Couple," because it combined the sophisticated Formula One driver with the grizzled veteran short-tracker.

Surprisingly to some, the pair hit it off from their first day of testing together in the spring, and instantly developed a respect and friendship.

Before his crash, Piquet had said he wanted to continue racing, but only at Indianapolis each year. After the month of May, he repeated his comments to ESPN's Derek Daly. But, he, too, would face months of recovery before a return to Indy would be a realistic thought.

For others, the blows were less severe. Roberto Guerrero had gotten his first "500" pole, only to have an accident in the preliminary laps while warming up his tires. Hiro Matsushita who crashed on Pole Day, recovered quickly and hopes to bring his Japanese support back for 1993.

Four-time winner Rick Mears crashed, and his bid for an unprecedented fifth victory would be delayed by another year. Both his record and his perseverance say he'll be back. Lightning-fast Jim Crawford, the tireless tester of the Buick engine, Emerson Fittipaldi and Arie Luyendyk would also have to wait another year. Their records and performances, too, establish them in advance as contenders.

Previous winners Gordon Johncock and Tom Sneva had short 1992 races. Fans remember the Johncock-Mears finish of 1982 and "The Gas Man" developed a large following by becoming the first driver to qualify at 200 miles an hour at Indy. Will the right deal, the right combination of car, driver and team, come together to bring them a taste of their past "500" glory?

Rookies Ted Prappas, Brian Bonner, Paul Tracy, Jimmy Vasser, Philippe Gache, Eric Bachelart and Rookie of the Year Lyn St. James are now veterans with their first Indianapolis 500 behind them.

And four-time winner A.J. Foyt, who finished ninth in his record

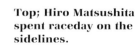

Top; Hiro Matsushita spent raceday on the sidelines.

Left; Indy veterans are already looking for the right deal in 1993.

AFTER THE ROAR

35th start, could return for a 36th. It is a record that may never be broken, one that had built a powerful image to race fans around the world.

Among them, other returning veterans and the 1993 crop of newcomers yet to be assigned their chance, a new story is already starting to unfold to continue the legend and legacy of the Indianapolis 500.

JOVY MARCELO, 1965-1992

Jovy Marcelo took the dream of becoming the first Filipino driver to ever start the Indianapolis 500 close to reality.

He had won the 1991 Formula Atlantic championship with victories at Lime Rock and Nazareth before contacting Euromotorsport team owner Antonio Ferrari about an Indy Car ride for 1992.

"He sent me a resume in November and we talked on the phone a couple of times," Ferrari said. "I was in Italy and he sent me a fax. I talked to maybe 20 drivers, but without actually seeing each other, we did the deal."

Marcelo made the jump to the PPG Cup ranks and first met Ferrari for a test at Indianapolis Raceway Park before the trip to Australia for the season opener.

"He showed he was a good test driver," Ferrari said. "He felt very well what was going on with the car. The nice thing about Jovy was, that when the car was right, he did fast laps. He didn't do fast laps just to be doing them. In qualifying in Australia, he was two full seconds faster than he'd practiced."

After Jovy crashed in practice at Phoenix, Ferrari stuck with him for Long Beach, then embarked on a vigorous testing and practice schedule at Indianapolis.

Marcelo passed his driver's test with flying colors, joining six other rookies in getting the okay on the first day of practice in May. But as he built up to speed on Friday, May 15, tragedy struck.

The 27-year-old driver went into turn #1 on his 548th practice lap of the month, did a three-quarter spin and hit the outside wall. He was pronounced dead of head injuries less than half an hour later at Methodist Hospital.

"I think with a testing program, which we had scheduled after Indy, he needed only miles," Ferrari said. "He was a professional driver, a professional man. Our car was second in miles overall at the time — I think (Emerson) Fittipaldi had 10 more laps than us.

"We didn't have maximum speed but we hadn't given him the 'wings' yet. We were up to maybe 217."

The tragic loss of the likable driver was a personal one for Ferrari.

"He became a very good friend of mine and stayed at my house when he came to Indy," the car owner said. "Jovy was learning, learning, learning every day."

Ferrari said plans were formulating to honor his memory in his home country by establishing a program in his name to bring other Filipino drivers to race in the United States.

"Jovy ran for his country," Ferrari said. "He liked the idea of representing the Philippines at Indy."

QUALIFYING AWARDS

PPG Pole Award - $100,000
PPG INDUSTRIES
Plus additional $5,000 and a Starcraft/Chevy van ($35,000 value)
STARCRAFT CORPORATION and CHEVROLET MOTOR DIVISION
Roberto Guerrero

GTE "Front Runner" Award - $30,000
$10,000 awarded to each front row driver
GTE NORTH, INC.
Roberto Guerrero, Eddie Cheever, Mario Andretti

Thomas Barrett "Fastest Qualifying Lap" Award - $10,000
THOMAS W. BARRETT III INC., Greatest Name in Classic Cars
Roberto Guerrero

Kenwood "On the Bubble" Award - $10,000
33rd fastest qualifier
KENWOOD U.S.A., CORPORATION
Ted Prappas

True Value "Master Mechanic" Award - $10,000
plus Lawn Chief Garden Tractor awarded to pole position chief mechanic
COTTER AND COMPANY
John Anderson

Ameritech PagesPlus® "Youngest Starting Driver" Award - $5,000
AMERITECH PUBLISHING, INC.
Paul Tracy

D.L. Clark Candy "Slo-Poke" Award - $5,000
awarded to driver posting the slowest single qualifying lap
D.L. CLARK CANDY
Jeff Andretti

Indiana Bell "First in the Field" Award - $5,000
INDIANA BELL
Arie Luyendyk

Jim Hurtubise/Monarch Beverage "Oldest Starting Driver" Award - $5,000
MONARCH BEVERAGE CO., INC.
A.J. Foyt, Jr.

NewsPager "Most Consistent Qualifying Laps" Award - $5,000
NEWSPAGER CORPORATION OF AMERICA
Bobby Rahal

Permatex "Fast Orange" Award - $5,000
awarded to the fastest qualifier
PERMATEX
Roberto Guerrero

S R E Industries "My Bubble Burst" Award - $5,000
awarded to first alternate at end of qualifying
S R E INDUSTRIES
Scott Goodyear

T.P. Donovan "Top Starting Rookie" Award - $5,000
OLINGER DISTRIBUTING CO.
Eric Bachelart

SPECIAL INCENTIVE AWARDS

AMERICAN DAIRY AWARDS
$9,750 - American Dairy Association
(winner, fastest rookie, winning
chief mechanic)
Al Unser Jr., Jimmy Vasser,
Owen Snyder

**BANK ONE, INDIANAPOLIS
"ROOKIE OF THE YEAR" AWARD**
$10,000 - Bank One, Indianapolis
Lyn St. James

BEAR "LEADER AT LAP 62" AWARD
$6,200 - Bear Automotive
Michael Andretti

BORG-WARNER TROPHY AWARD
$100,000 plus trophy replica
Borg-Warner
Al Unser Jr.

**CADILLAC OFFICIAL
PACE CAR AWARD**
1992 Cadillac Allanté Official
Pace Car
Al Unser Jr.

**CHAPMAN S. ROOT
MEMORIAL AWARD**
$5,000 - Terre Haute First
National Bank
Arie Luyendyk, leader at lap 48

**CLINT BRAWNER MECHANICAL
EXCELLENCE AWARD**
$5,000 - Clint Brawner Mechanical
Excellence Award Foundation
Bernie Myers

**DEERING CLEANERS
"WORKHORSE" AWARD**
$5,000 - Richard Deering
Cleaners, Inc.
Paul Tracy, most practice laps

**GILLETTE
"HALFWAY CHALLENGE"**
$10,000 - Gillette Company
Michael Andretti, leader at
the halfway point

**GOODYEAR
"WINNING CAR OWNER" AWARD**
$5,000 plus ring - The Goodyear Tire &
Rubber Co.
Rick Galles, Maury Kraines

**HERFF JONES
"CHAMPION OF CHAMPIONS"**
$10,000 plus winner's ring
Herff Jones
Al Unser Jr.

**HINCKLEY &SCHMITT
HOOSIER BOTTLED WATER
"ENDURANCE" AWARD**
$5,000 - Hinckley & Schmitt, Inc.
(lowest placed finisher running
at the finish)
Dominic Dobson

IBM "FASTEST LAP" AWARD
$10,000 - IBM Corporation
Michael Andretti, fastest race lap

**INB "LEADERS'
CIRCLE" AWARD**
$10,000 - INB National Bank
Michael Andretti, leader of most
race laps

**INDIANA GAS
"ON THE GAS" AWARD**
$5,000 - Indiana Gas Company, Inc.
Michael Andretti, leader at lap 5

**INDIANA OXYGEN
"PERSEVERANCE"AWARD**
$5,000 - Indiana Oxygen
Lyn St. James

**JCPENNEY "500"
WINNER QUILT AWARD**
$5,000 and quilt by Jeanetta
Holder - JCPenney
Al Unser Jr.

**KODAK
"PHOTO FINISH" AWARD**
$7,500 - Eastman Kodak Company
Al Unser Jr., race winner

CONTINGENCY AWARDS

AMWAY FREEDOM SYNTHETIC OIL
$15,000

AMWAY FREEDOM FUEL ADDITIVE
$15,000

BELL HELMETS
$6,000

ROBERT BOSCH CORPORATION
$25,000

CANON, U.S.A.
$7,500

CHAMPION SPARK PLUG COMPANY
$50,000

CHEVROLET
$5,000

CONOCO INC.
$10,000

CRAFTSMAN TRACTORS
$5,000

DELCO REMY, GMC
$15,500

EARL'S PERFORMANCE PRODUCTS
$10,500

FIRST BRANDS - STP RACING
$20,000

HYPERCO, INC.
$5,000

IDEAL DIVISION/STANT CORP.
$5,000

LOCTITE CORPORATION
$22,500

MALLORY INC.
$5,000

MANCO, INC.
$25,000

MOBIL OIL CORPORATION
$5,000

MONROE AUTO EQUIPMENT
$5,000

PPG INDUSTRIES, INC.
$330,000

PENNZOIL PRODUCTS COMPANY
$5,000

PETRON INTERNATIONAL, INC.
$5,000

PREMIER INDUSTRIAL CORP.
$10,000

QUAKER STATE OIL REFINING CORP.
$5,000

RAYBESTOS/BRAKE PARTS, INC.
$20,000

SEARS DIEHARD BATTERY
$15,500

SIMPSON RACE PRODUCTS
$5,000

SNAP-ON TOOLS
$5,000

STANT MANUFACTURING, INC.
$5,000

TEXACO LUBRICANT COMPANY
$5,000

TOTAL PETROLEUM
$5,000

VALVOLINE, INC.
$25,000

UNITED STATES AUTO CLUB — OFFICERS AND RACE STAFF

USAC OFFICERS & EXECUTIVE OFFICIALS

Robert G. Moorhead, Chairman of the Board; Richard King, President; Roger McCluskey, Executive Vice President and Director of Competition; Robert Cassaday, Vice President, Steward and Chief Registrar; Bill Marvel, Vice President; Gary Sokola, Deputy Competition Director; Tommy Hunt, Vice President; Dick Jordan, Communications Director; Donald Davidson, Statistician and Historian; Ron Green, Membership Director; Thomas W. Binford, Chief Steward; Arthur D. Meyers, Steward; Rich Coy, Steward and Director of Product Certification; Keith Ward, Steward; Art Graham, Director of Timing and Scoring; Duane Sweeney, Chief Starter; Bill Carey, Assistant Starter; Jack Beckley, Technical Advisor.

USAC TECHNICAL SUPERVISORS

Mike Devin, Technical Director; Don McGregor, Jerry Grobe, Deputy Directors; Dennis Hunley, Deputy Director NDT & Metallurgical Committee. Samuel Burge, Richard Gunder, Ray Linton, D. Ray Marshall, Mike Smith and William Sparks, Supervisors; Andy Anderson, Jack Jenkins, Steve Jordan, David Kyle, Ben Lawrence, Ray Macht, Pat Martin, Marcel Periat, Dick Plageman, Ron Scudder, Russ Stone, William Teeguarden, Jeff Van Treese, Jon Van Treese and Paul Wells, Vice Chairmen.

USAC TECHNICAL ASSISTANTS

Dennis Brankle, Gary Brewer, Lila Brewer, Jeff Collins, Bud Edwards, Nancy Marshall, Tom Miller, Kevin Park, Paul Park, Sandy Park, Steve Park, Bruce Parsell, Mike Reffitt, Dave Simpson, Larry Stubbs, Race Spec Inspection; E. Budy, Jr., B. Collins, J. Freeze, J. Hunley, S. Hunley, C. Kiracofe, J. Knavel, S. Kontney, T.L. Kontney, C. Majors, M. McLaughlin, B. Messer, G. Monks, H. Rohm, Jr., C. Small, L. Snyder, W. Tarpley, D. Taylor and C. Trotter, NonDestructive Testing; Dave King, Communications; Harry Robertson, Fuel Cell Advisor; Ray Carpenter and Terry Haley, Assistant Weigh Masters; Ann Grobe, Pat McCarty, Vicky Ray, Martha Shields and Toni Sylvester, Technical Data; F. Adams, A. Adastik, A. Albrecht, D. Anderson, A. Ankerman, P. Asa, H. Baker, J. Baker, D. Barrett, S. Bell, A. Biggs, R. Bivens, G. Bloeser, F. Boling, J. Bornhorst, W. Brizius, F. Burdette, R. Butterfield, P. Cannaley, R. Carson, J. Clark, V. Clossin, B. Clough, F. Collins, J. Cowley, D. Cox, C. Curry, F. Dochnal, W. Dunkerson, D. Dunning, A. Edgar, K. Edwards, R. Elsner, B. Fahey, J. Fearson, J. Fielder, C. Fielder, C. Fischer, G. Frashier, J. Fullan, J.M. Grobe, J.W. Grobe, R. Gorbe, R. Hanson, C. Harmon, C. Hartzer, E. Held, D. Herling, W. Hittenberger, J. Innis, J. Jenkins, J. Johnson, J. Keith, J. King, W. Koleta, K. Krimmel, S. Lewis, B. Lockwood, D. Love, J. Maher, J. Mayhew, H. Merritt, M. Milharcik, J. Muller, R. Murphy, R. Nicoloff, J. Nims, C. Parmelli, S. Pelsor, A. Pickett, R. Price, M. Ray, D. Riffel, B. Runyon, M. Sandler, A. Schmidt, M. Selode, N. Shields, B. Smith, J. Smith, K. Smith, F. Snow, F. Stewart, W. Strong, T. Taylor, B. Turner, R. Van Note, D. Verrill, A. Vesely, W. Wacker, C. Wasdyke, R. White, P. Wilson, G. Yohe, Technical Observers.

USAC OBSERVERS

Claude Fisher, Chief Observer; Edwin Board, Ted Lake, John Notte III and Robert Stanley, Deputy Chief Observers; Dennis Barker, Jim Best, Jeff Boles, Butch Bundrandt, Richard Eiler, Gary Goodrich, Rick Hoehnke, Mike Lake, Jim Nell, Jr., Walter Schroeder and Glenn Timmis, Assistant Chief Observers.

OBSERVERS

S. Amos, J. Bailey, A. Barker, R.J. Barron, R.N. Barron, M. Bennett, N. Bennett, R. Bentley, Jr., R. Best, T. Blanchard, W. Borecki, J. Boucher, J. Brasker, R. Brown, F. Bruckner, J. Butler, L. Cheatham, R. Clark, S. Coomes, M. Cox, R. Cox, Jr., V. Dentice, D. Distler, J. Dudley, G. Edwards, D. Fox, F. Frost, J. Gilette, D. Goonen, R. Hamilton, J. Hanna, J. Haynes, J. Highsmith, R. Hogan, G. Humphrey, C. Hurt, L. Hurt, P. Johnson, S. Knoy, K. Kruty, L. Kunkle, F. Kurtz, D. Lanham, N. Legamoff, R. Ledbetter, J. Leser, Jr., L. Leser, W. Loucks, R. Maas, P. Manuel, B. Morna, E. Motsinger, J. Nell III, P. Panhorst, G. Parsons, K. Perkins, D. Price, J. Randolph, K. Ruddick, R. Rude, J. Schaffner, R. Schroeder, G. Schultz, S. Schultz, J. Schwomeyer, B. Sewell, J. Simko, G. Snider, J. Snider, T. Stawicki, C. Steele, R. Stoddard, E. Sweeney, M. Sweeney, R. Tharp, D. Thompson, M. Thompson, R. Vannice, G. Werner, P. Whalen, G. Wirey, E. Wright, T. Wyn, Observers.

USAC CERTIFICATION COMMITTEE

Rich Coy, Director, Product Certification; William Conley, Deputy Director; Frank Wilhelm, Deputy Director; D. Cherry, C. Colip, R. Condit, S. Ingle, A. Johnson, D. Kischell, J. Locke, G. Mayfield, D. Nicely, T. Vastine, Vice Chairmen.

USAC SAFETY OFFICIALS

John Gilmore, Director; Robert Nolen, Deputy Director.

USAC TIMING & SCORING OFFICIALS

Art Graham, Director; Les Kimbrell, Director of Scoring Operations; Larry Allen, Chief Scoring Technician; Jerry L. Challis, Chief Scorer; Dennis Dyer, Chief Scoring Engineer; Andrew Graham, Chief of Scoring Systems; Harold Hamilton, Chief Timing Engineer; Kay Kimbrell, Chief Serial Scorer; Jack Taylor, Chief Scoring Observer; Ron Vogt, Chief Pit Scorer; Dick Webb, Chief Auditor; Chuck Whetsel, Chief Scoring Judge; Bert Wilkerson, Chief of Scoring Equipment; Mike Cramer, Scoring Registrar; Ray House, Chief Timer Emeritus; Bob Lohman, Honorary Chief Scorer; C.J. Christy, Honorary Chief Timer.

TIMING & SCORING STAFF

Jim Akers, Bill Ballard, Jr., Dave Batson, Dave Berryman, Ken Blackburn, Chap Blackwell III, Andy Blahut, Bob Blahut, Bill Bodin, Barbara Bucher, Bob Cole, Susie Ebershoff-Coles, Wayne Coles, Joyce Diemer, Patrick Diemer, Mayo Ellis, Linda Foster, Norm Funkhouser, Michael Gray, Bob Hicks, Randy Hoover, Ryan Hoover, Susan Hoover, Lisa Lengerich, Larry Martin, Bob Mount, Craig Newman, Gary Paschke, Kevin Paschke, Ray Paschke, Larry Potter, Nick Reed, Bill Reeser, Dave Rogers, Bill Spellerberg, Bill Stevens, Don Stone, Ed Tate, Dave Tobias, George Vogelsperger, Craig Wambold, Don Wilkerson, Bert Wilkerson II, Pete Woytovech, Chuck Yoder, Lenny Zwik.
DATA-1 SUPPORT STAFF: Ian Chatwin, Director; Chris Gamgee, Ed Witte.
IBM SYSTEMS SUPPORT STAFF: John Mann, Director; Kathye Beagan, Pat Bowlds, Rick Hughes, Tom Murphy, Ray Szeluga (Lexmark).

ADDITIONAL RACE DAY PERSONNEL

L. Albean, B. Alexander, B. Armbruster, L. Ashburn, J. Baden, B. Ballard III, J. Bertholf, C. Blackwell IV, S. Blank, C. Brethman, R. Bromwell, B. Campbell, D. Campbell, D. Challis, B. Chasteen, L. Crane, S. Crane, S. Demeter, R. Fegan, D. Fisher, B. Gardner, D.J. Garrision, D. Graham, S. Gray, S. Griffith, R. Hanes, G. Harabin, L. Harabin, R. Harvey, N. Hastings, S. Holt, B. Hunter, D. Hunter, P. Karle, R. Kenyon, J. Lane, E. Leduke, B. Lindholm, J. Lindholm, E. Long, J. Lynch, C. Macomber, T. McKinney, L. Mitchell, L. Mitchell, B. Mooney, H. Moore, C. Moorman, J. Morphy, B. Moyer, A. Neuner, S. Oliver, L. Olson, D. Paisley, C. Parrott, J. Paschke, Jeff Perkins, Jim Perkins, John Perkins, D. Petrali, J. Pingle, T. Premici, F. Raymundo, J. Reed, D. Renzoni, R. Renzoni, B. Reynolds, D. Richey, E. Rodman, D. Rutledge, C. Schendel, J. Schuh, M. Sedam, D. Smiley, S. Steele, R. Stone, Jeff Taylor, R. Thompson, C. Tunny, L. Vastine, Greg Vogelsperger, S. Voorhees, B. Weir, S. Wright, J. Youngblood.

Trackside Computing by the IBM PS/2, the Official Computer of the United States Auto Club

Data Processing Services courtesy of IBM INDIANA

Publishing Services courtesy of KINKO'S COPIES of Lafayette Square

BOARD OF SAFETY

Lloyd R. Jennings, Supt., State Police; Joseph G. McAtee, Sheriff, Marion County; James D. Toler, Chief, Indianapolis Police Dept.; and Jeffrey L. Dine, Chief, Speedway Police Dept.

CHAPLAINS

Rev. Michael Welch and Dr. Andrew P. Crowley.

MISCELLANEOUS

Supervisor of Track Fire Prevention - Jack Gilmore; Score Board Manager - Homer Taylor; Chief Announcer - Tom Carnegie; Telephone Service - Indiana Bell Co. and AT&T; Wrecker Service - No*Mar Towing Equipment; Wheel Aligning and Balancing Service - Bear; and Welding Service - Indiana Oxygen Company.

MEDICAL STAFF & SUPPORT

Administrative Staff: Bruce B. Cross, Robert C. Held, Mike Miles; Executive Secretary, Mary Simpson; Nursing Director, Terri Cordell, R.N.; Assistant Nursing Directors: Roxanne Coats, R.N., Lisa Miller, R.N.; Emergency Medical Services Coordinator, Andrew Bowles; Optometrist, E. Jerome Babitz, O.D.; Medical Director, Henry Bock, M.D.; Assistant Medical Director, Brent Furbee, M.D.; Laboratory and Cardiology Consultants: Methodist Hospital; Emergency Helicopter Service - MBB Helicopter Corp., Methodist Life Line, H.H. Gregg; Medical Electronics: Hewlett Packard, Physio-Control, IVAC, Marquette, Laerdal.

1992 DAILY PRACTICE LAPS

Car No.	Driver	Yr./Ch. Eng.	Sa 2	Su 3	Mo 4	Tu 5	We 6	Th 7	Fr 8	Sa 9	Su 10	Mo 11	Tu 12	We 13	Th 14	Fr 15	Sa 16	Su 17	Th 21	Total Laps	Driver
1	Michael Andretti	92/L/FC	—	14	42	20	32	39	3	14	22	—	—	—	—	—	—	—	23	209	Andretti, Michael
1T	Michael Andretti	92/L/FC	—	—	—	—	11	—	—	—	—	—	20	49	8	92	—	—	—	181	Andretti, Michael
2	Mario Andretti	92/L/FC	—	36	41	59	39	59	20	31	—	21	—	—	—	—	—	—	23	329	Andretti, Mario
2T	Mario Andretti	92/L/FC	—	—	—	—	—	—	11	—	—	54	—	43	36	55	—	—	—	199	Andretti, Mario
3	Al Unser, Jr.	92/G/CA	13	60	80	41	45	50	45	32	—	14	—	—	—	—	—	—	30	410	Unser Jr., Al
3T	Al Unser, Jr	92/G/CA	—	—	—	17	—	—	—	—	—	21	12	85	24	77	—	—	—	236	Unser Jr., Al
4	Rick Mears	92/P/CB	—	57	62	64	12	—	15	28	—	—	—	—	—	—	—	—	32	270	Mears, Rick
4T	Rick Mears	91/P/CB	20	—	—	—	9	—	—	—	—	—	—	—	—	—	—	—	—	29	Mears, Rick
5	Emerson Fittipaldi	92/P/CB	—	70	48	72	52	47	16	36	—	79	25	75	59	—	—	—	24	603	Fittipaldi, Emerson
5T	Emerson Fittipaldi	92/P/CB	25	—	—	—	—	—	—	—	—	—	—	—	—	—	—	—	—	25	Fittipaldi, Emerson
5T	Paul Tracy	92/P/CB	—	—	—	—	—	—	19	—	—	17	25	—	—	—	43	—	—	104	Tracy, Paul
6	Arie Luyendyk	92/L/FC	—	—	36	37	21	58	43	32	—	—	—	35	36	68	47	—	27	440	Luyendyk, Arie
7	Paul Tracy	91/P/CA	68	—	—	68	—	16	47	39	—	61	—	114	73	—	—	—	34	520	Tracy, Paul
7T	Rick Mears	92/P/CA	—	—	—	—	—	—	—	—	—	—	—	12	44	45	55	—	—	156	Mears, Rick
7T	Paul Tracy	92/P/CA	—	—	—	—	—	—	—	—	—	—	—	—	—	—	—	22	—	22	Tracy, Paul
7T	Emerson Fittipaldi	92/P/CA	11	—	—	—	—	—	—	—	—	—	—	—	—	—	—	—	—	11	Fittipaldi, Emerson
7T	Rick Mears	92/P/CA	36	—	—	—	—	—	—	—	—	—	—	—	—	—	—	—	—	36	Mears, Rick
7T	Paul Tracy	91/P/CA	—	194	—	3	—	—	—	—	—	—	—	—	—	—	—	—	—	197	Tracy, Paul
8	John Andretti	92/L/CA	28	57	1	48	73	—	38	10	—	—	—	—	—	—	—	—	31	286	Andretti, John
8T	John Andretti	92/L/CA	—	—	69	—	—	55	19	31	—	11	—	52	60	19	—	—	—	316	Andretti, John
9	Eddie Cheever	92/L/FC	8	48	38	61	71	8	47	40	31	—	—	65	—	98	41	—	23	579	Cheever, Eddie
10	Scott Pruett	92/T/CA	—	—	—	14	65	45	35	37	—	84	29	54	—	—	—	—	26	389	Pruett, Scott
10T	Scott Pruett	92/T/CA	—	63	60	—	—	—	—	—	19	—	—	—	—	—	—	—	—	142	Pruett, Scott
11	Raul Boesel	92/L/CA	—	—	—	—	—	—	—	—	82	43	—	11	—	—	—	—	21	157	Boesel, Raul
11	Hiro Matsushita	92/L/CA	—	36	67	70	22	44	—	—	—	—	—	—	—	—	—	—	—	239	Matsushita, Hiro
11T	Hiro Matsushita	92/L/CA	—	—	49	—	—	—	25	17	—	—	—	—	—	—	—	—	—	91	Matsushita, Hiro
12	Bobby Rahal	92/L/CA	29	35	85	54	37	56	44	35	—	—	—	—	—	—	—	—	20	395	Rahal, Bobby
12T	Bobby Rahal	92/L/CA	—	—	—	18	20	12	—	—	—	16	32	57	62	39	67	23	—	356	Rahal, Bobby
14	A.J. Foyt	92/L/CA	—	—	—	—	17	29	34	31	10	8	—	42	—	—	13	21	24	229	Foyt, A.J.
14T	Jeff Andretti	91/L/CA	—	—	—	—	—	—	—	—	—	—	—	—	—	34	24	81	—	139	Andretti, Jeff
15	Scott Goodyear	92/L/CA	—	50	72	29	11	44	84	17	33	26	4	—	—	—	—	—	38	420	Goodyear, Scott
15	Mike Groff	92/L/CA	—	—	—	—	—	—	—	—	—	—	—	—	—	—	10	27	—	37	Groff, Mike
15T	Scott Goodyear	91/L/CA	—	21	—	—	43	8	—	21	—	—	—	—	34	—	—	—	—	127	Goodyear, Scott
15T	Mike Groff	91/L/CA	—	—	—	—	—	—	—	—	—	—	—	—	—	52	—	—	9	61	Groff, Mike
16	Tony Bettenhausen	91/P/CA	50	16	34	5	5	—	—	—	3	—	—	—	—	—	—	—	—	113	Bettenhausen, T.
16T	Tony Bettenhausen	91/P/CA	—	2	25	—	57	51	44	33	—	—	—	73	74	79	67	80	—	585	Bettenhausen, T.
17	Mike Groff	91/L/CA	—	—	—	—	—	—	—	—	—	—	—	—	—	—	28	—	—	28	Groff, Mike
17	Johnny Rutherford	91/L/CA	—	—	—	—	—	—	—	—	—	—	—	—	—	32	97	67	—	196	Rutherford, Johnny
18	Danny Sullivan	92/G/CA	28	42	32	66	49	58	67	31	28	—	—	—	—	—	11	—	29	438	Sullivan, Danny
18T	Danny Sullivan	91/G/CA	—	15	—	—	—	—	—	—	—	—	—	39	39	48	—	—	—	141	Sullivan, Danny
19	Eric Bachelart	90/L/B	—	—	—	—	—	—	—	—	—	—	—	—	—	—	17	19	—	36	Bachelart, Eric
19	Brian Bonner	90/L/B	—	—	—	36	—	—	—	—	—	—	—	—	—	—	—	—	—	36	Bonner, Brian
21	Buddy Lazier	91/L/B	—	—	52	35	37	33	29	36	37	—	—	32	—	—	—	—	26	317	Lazier, Buddy

1992 DAILY PRACTICE LAPS

Car No.	Driver	Yr./Ch. Eng.	Sa 2	Su 3	Mo 4	Tu 5	We 6	Th 7	Fr 8	Sa 9	Su 10	Mo 11	Tu 12	We 13	Th 14	Fr 15	Sa 16	Su 17	Th 21	Total Laps	Driver
21T	Buddy Lazier	90/L/B	—	—	—	—	—	—	—	—	—	—	—	—	—	9	12	—	—	21	Lazier, Buddy
22	Scott Brayton	92/L/CA	63	20	15	—	—	—	—	—	—	—	—	—	—	—	—	—	—	98	Brayton, Scott
22T	Scott Brayton	92/L/B	—	28	48	23	—	29	71	31	—	35	—	46	33	—	—	—	31	375	Brayton, Scott
26	Jim Crawford	92/L/B	14	—	20	—	24	20	23	7	36	—	8	51	40	77	—	—	28	348	Crawford, Jim
27	Nelson Piquet	92/L/B	25	37	43	27	46	32	—	—	—	—	—	—	—	—	—	—	—	210	Piquet, Nelson
27T	Gary Bettenhausen	92/L/B	—	—	—	—	—	—	11	—	21	—	—	—	—	—	—	—	—	32	Bettenhausen, G.
27T	Al Unser	92/L/B	—	—	—	—	—	—	—	—	47	1	20	23	31	—	—	11	17	150	Unser, Al
30	Fabrizio Barbazza	90/L/B	23	31	—	—	—	—	—	22	62	—	—	—	—	—	—	—	—	138	Barbazza, Fabrizio
30	Johnny Parsons	90/L/B	—	—	—	—	—	—	—	—	—	—	—	—	—	24	53	48	—	125	Parsons, Johnny
31	Ted Prappas	91/L/CA	—	40	38	39	43	—	32	26	22	—	—	34	15	—	32	46	18	385	Prappas, Ted
34	Jeff Wood	91/L/B	—	—	—	—	22	31	47	10	54	49	16	52	8	—	40	60	—	389	Wood, Jeff
36	Roberto Guerrero	92/L/B	14	27	20	41	36	34	12	27	—	—	17	72	35	—	—	—	21	356	Guerrero, Roberto
36To	Roberto Guerrero	92/L/B	—	—	—	—	—	—	—	—	—	—	—	—	—	19	—	—	—	19	Guerrero, Roberto
38	John Andretti	91/L/CA	30	24	—	—	—	—	—	—	9	—	—	—	—	—	—	—	—	63	Andretti, John
38	Didier Theys	91/L/CA	—	—	—	—	—	—	—	—	35	32	13	51	49	63	58	91	—	392	Theys, Didier
39	Brian Bonner	91/L/B	—	—	—	—	—	—	—	—	—	—	7	30	76	107	40	—	31	291	Bonner, Brian
42	Fabrizio Barbazza	91/L/CW	—	—	—	—	—	—	—	—	—	—	—	—	—	14	—	—	—	14	Barbazza, Fabrizio
44	Philippe Gache	91/L/CA	27	62	17	52	—	29	29	—	—	48	—	—	—	—	—	—	23	287	Gache, Philippe
44T	Philippe Gache	91/L/CA	36	—	—	—	56	—	32	—	—	—	—	—	—	—	2	—	—	126	Gache, Philippe
47	Jimmy Vasser	91/L/CA	—	—	—	—	39	35	32	29	39	—	—	—	—	—	—	—	—	174	Vasser, Jimmy
47T	Jimmy Vasser	91/L/CA	68	46	33	—	—	—	—	—	—	—	18	58	—	—	26	30	35	314	Vasser, Jimmy
48	Jeff Andretti	91/L/CA	—	—	13	48	15	56	4	30	—	55	29	17	44	—	—	—	32	343	Andretti, Jeff
50	Jovy Marcelo	91/L/CW	61	69	40	24	—	—	37	20	62	77	39	71	41	5	—	—	—	546	Marcelo, Jovy
51	Gary Bettenhausen	92/L/B	24	48	50	53	70	39	33	31	—	36	20	72	19	—	—	14	32	541	Bettenhausen, G.
51T	Nelson Piquet	92/L/B	31	—	—	—	—	—	—	—	—	—	—	—	—	—	—	—	—	31	Piquet, Nelson
59	Gary Bettenhausen	91/L/B	27	—	—	—	—	—	—	—	—	—	—	—	—	25	—	—	—	52	Bettenhausen, G.
59	Rocky Moran	91/L/B	—	—	—	—	—	—	—	—	—	—	—	—	—	6	—	—	—	6	Moran, Rocky
59	Tom Sneva	91/L/B	—	—	—	—	—	—	—	—	—	—	—	—	—	—	45	34	17	96	Sneva, Tom
61	Tony Bettenhausen	90/P/CA	—	—	—	—	—	—	—	—	—	—	—	12	—	—	—	—	—	12	Bettenhausen, T.
66	Mark Dismore	90/L/B	30	38	9	22	30	54	28	—	9	49	17	40	—	26	58	18	—	428	Dismore, Mark
68	Dominic Dobson	91/L/CA	—	30	—	—	—	—	—	—	48	—	—	57	—	—	35	22	28	190	Dobson, Dominic
81	Pancho Carter	91/L/B	—	—	—	—	—	—	—	—	—	—	—	16	21	—	34	—	—	71	Carter, Pancho
88	Kenji Momota	91/L/CA	47	44	44	—	42	—	—	—	—	—	—	—	2	54	51	34	—	318	Momota, Kenji
90	Lyn St. James	91/L/CW	45	69	51	11	65	29	48	36	59	—	—	35	7	28	9	—	—	492	St. James, Lyn
90	Lyn St. James	91/L/CA	—	—	—	—	—	—	—	—	—	—	—	—	—	—	27	27	27	100	St. James, Lyn
91	Stan Fox	91/L/B	—	11	33	—	—	—	—	—	—	4	—	43	—	—	—	7	12	111	Fox, Stan
91T	Stan Fox	91/L/B	31	16	25	—	21	17	24	19	—	14	14	—	17	—	—	—	19	205	Fox, Stan
92	Gordon Johncock	91/L/B	—	—	—	—	23	15	67	30	48	14	33	14	35	67	73	50	19	488	Johncock, Gordon
92T	Gordon Johncock	91/L/B	—	30	—	—	—	—	—	—	—	—	—	—	30	—	—	6	—	66	Johncock, Gordon
93	Mark Dismore	90/L/B	—	—	—	—	—	—	—	—	—	—	—	—	—	—	—	70	—	70	Dismore, Mark
93	John Paul, Jr.	90/L/B	39	35	—	—	—	41	37	—	—	10	—	—	—	—	—	—	16	178	Paul Jr., John
93T	John Paul, Jr.	90/L/B	—	—	47	14	23	8	39	34	—	11	—	64	26	—	—	20	16	286	Paul Jr., John

1992 DAILY BEST SPEEDS

Car No. Driver	Yr./Ch. Eng.	Sa 2	Su 3	Mo 4	Tu 5	We 6	Th 7	Fr 8	Sa 9	Su 10	Mo 11	Tu 12	We 13	Th 14	Fr 15	Sa 16	Su 17	Th 21	Driver
1 Michael Andretti	92/L/FC	226.187		230.852	229.879	231.535	232.013	160.088	231.178	229.048								225.220	Andretti, Michael
1T Michael Andretti	92/L/FC					219.753						229.950	227.883	229.674	229.329				Andretti, Michael
2 Mario Andretti	92/L/FC		224.713	229.504	229.990	231.124	229.673	233.203	230.863		224.210							226.409	Andretti, Mario
2T Mario Andretti	92/L/FC							229.475			225.604		226.740	228.131	228.444				Andretti, Mario
3 Al Unser, Jr.	92/G/CA	211.695	220.507	223.403	227.249	224.786	224.399	228.056	224.550		211.810							212.169	Unser Jr., Al
3T Al Unser, Jr	92/G/CA				221.943						215.188	217.344	216.841	215.595	217.934				Unser Jr., Al
4 Rick Mears	92/P/CB		220.935	226.273	225.932	222.557		220.907	225.496									221.708	Mears, Rick
4T Rick Mears	91/P/CB	220.740				213.310													Mears, Rick
5 Emerson Fittipaldi	92/P/CB		224.159	224.467	224.983	222.430	225.886	221.827	225.937		224.725	225.575	221.081	226.729				222.949	Fittipaldi, Emerson
5T Emerson Fittipaldi	92/P/CB	218.208																	Fittipaldi, Emerson
5T Paul Tracy	92/P/CB						215.863				216.962	222.316				219.143			Tracy, Paul
6 Arie Luyendyk	92/L/FC			218.935	228.079	228.004	230.084	232.654	230.881				224.126	224.411	226.290	226.620		225.423	Luyendyk, Arie
7 Paul Tracy	91/P/CA	219.138			222.766	217.108		222.425	221.298				222.222	222.030				217.702	Tracy, Paul
7T Rick Mears	92/P/CA										223.586		203.339	223.580	222.524	220.984			Mears, Rick
7T Paul Tracy	92/P/CA																221.528		Tracy, Paul
7T Emerson Fittipaldi	92/P/CA	212.369																	Fittipaldi, Emerson
7T Rick Mears	92/P/CA	220.615																	Mears, Rick
7T Paul Tracy	91/P/CA	222.596			131.266														Tracy, Paul
8 John Andretti	92/L/CA	222.047	221.511	82.871	225.056	225.586		225.705	222.711									221.446	Andretti, John
8T John Andretti	92/L/CA			224.517			226.056	226.187	228.920		210.384		221.479	221.965	220.826				Andretti, John
9 Eddie Cheever	92/L/FC	191.286	221.043	219.829	227.894	229.550	220.377	228.443	229.305	230.971			225.124		227.152	224.349		224.921	Cheever, Eddie
10 Scott Pruett	92/T/CA				222.700	224.048	221.554	223.491	221.434		216.826	217.323	214.357					213.660	Pruett, Scott
10T Scott Pruett	92/T/CA		217.302	219.711			11.614	214.311											Pruett, Scott
11 Raul Boesel	92/L/CA									222.750	217.581		216.440					218.452	Boesel, Raul
11 Hiro Matsushita	92/L/CA			216.138	223.026	216.794	224.232												Matsushita, Hiro
11T Hiro Matsushita	92/L/CA	209.927						223.908	220.701										Matsushita, Hiro
12 Bobby Rahal	92/L/CA		221.103	223.641	225.078	224.691	226.227	228.432	226.346		217.897	223.336	221.027	221.321	221.844	221.136		223.336	Rahal, Bobby
12T Bobby Rahal	92/L/CA			215.548	220.296	220.453	222.200										219.469		Rahal, Bobby
14 A.J. Foyt	92/L/CA					214.260	221.173	223.430	223.680		215.807	223.336	219.015			210.546	220.006	215.957	Foyt, A.J.
14T Jeff Andretti	91/L/CA														213.048	216.019	217.749		Andretti, Jeff
15 Scott Goodyear	92/L/CA		219.555	223.758	224.321	220.712	218.160	224.131	221.228						192.094	220.967	217.376	219.181	Goodyear, Scott
15 Mike Groff	92/L/CA									223.109	221.844	133.042							Groff, Mike
15T Scott Goodyear	91/L/CA	210.163														222.041			Goodyear, Scott
15T Mike Groff	91/L/CA					221.883	218.113		220.097					218.394					Groff, Mike
16 Tony Bettenhausen	91/P/CA	217.918	217.202	220.157	208.126	220.275	219.855	213.974	218.605				215.765	219.904	221.033	217.402			Bettenhausen, T.
16T Tony Bettenhausen	91/P/CA		150.000	222.431		211.356				154.326					216.455	217.033			Bettenhausen, T.
17 Mike Groff	91/L/CA																217.760		Groff, Mike
17 Johnny Rutherford	91/L/CA		-												205.841		217.686		Rutherford, Johnny
18 Danny Sullivan	92/G/CA	210.817	215.936	218.087	222.932	221.380	221.893	224.042	220.334	225.383				221.866	212.831	214.674		214.608	Sullivan, Danny
18T Danny Sullivan	91/G/CA	206.195											210.995		219.786	211.566			Sullivan, Danny
19 Eric Bachelart	90/L/B	211.785	210.966	222.310		222.189	222.656	221.992					222.816	222.189	220.816	216.409	215.646	214.255	Bachelart, Eric

1992 DAILY BEST SPEEDS

Car No.	Driver	Yr./Ch. Eng.	Sa 2	Su 3	Mo 4	Tu 5	We 6	Th 7	Fr 8	Sa 9	Su 10	Mo 11	Tu 12	We 13	Th 14	Fr 15	Sa 16	Su 17	Th 21
19	Brian Bonner	90/L/B				209.732													
21	Buddy Lazier	91/L/B			215.884	219.549	220.534	222.216	223.220	222.299	223.120			221.168					213.965
21T	Buddy Lazier	90/L/B														155.602	201.126		
22	Scott Brayton	92/L/CA	224.065	220.783	221.022														
22T	Scott Brayton	92/L/B		223.093	227.468	227.646		220.431	224.455	227.848		220.783			218.840	224.232			223.187
26	Jim Crawford	92/L/B	229.609		233.433		233.239	229.515	231.344	220.886	229.113		223.953	223.569	227.606	226.193			218.378
27	Nelson Piquet	92/L/B	225.875	225.677	226.809	227.571	227.479	228.571	221.244										
27T	Gary Bettenhausen	92/L/B									220.366								
27T	Al Unser	92/L/B									224.372	16.656	223.375	213.518	220.957			217.439	217.570
30	Fabrizio Barbazza	90/L/B	202.776	207.297						212.049									
30	Johnny Parsons	90/L/B									220.308					207.934	215.621	216.747	
31	Ted Prappas	91/L/CA			206.996	214.367	216.107	217.648		219.218	213.452		216.388		221.212		217.591	219.432	212.114
34	Jeff Wood	91/L/B				215.388	201.554	205.156	206.426	198.873	209.355	216.050	215.481	214.194	210.975		204.453	210.783	
36	Roberto Guerrero	92/L/B	225.242	226.034	230.432	230.149	231.558	232.624	231.660	232.618			230.368	226.153	227.198				224.899
36T	Roberto Guerrero	92/L/B														215.260			
38	John Andretti	91/L/CA	213.939	215.095							194.780								
38	Didier Theys	91/L/CA									211.934	214.505	216.247	213.675	216.831	220.146	219.861	219.469	
39	Brian Bonner	91/L/B											111.295	210.374	211.426	215.332	221.255		209.298
42	Fabrizio Barbazza	91/L/CW														211.010			
44	Philippe Gache	91/L/CA		218.145	219.716	219.245				223.719		217.423							215.750
44T	Philippe Gache	91/L/CA		211.322		221.838	221.888	224.809		221.800							55.805		
47	Jimmy Vasser	91/L/CA					219.979	221.997	222.844	218.372	219.362								
47T	Jimmy Vasser	91/L/CA	218.978	216.351	221.719								216.388	221.675			221.304	222.469	217.728
48	Jeff Andretti	91/L/CA		214.941		223.375	220.065	220.210	134.467	221.070		215.817	214.276	211.431	219.796				208.478
50	Jovy Marcelo	91/L/CW	203.519	208.885		208.415			214.193	213.214	211.924	215.275	216.534	210.812	216.878	172.328			
51	Gary Bettenhausen	92/L/B	222.574	223.392	228.490	228.588	227.917	228.241	227.663	229.317		223.098	220.415	221.604	223.087			217.638	223.842
51T	Nelson Piquet	92/L/B	213.488																
59	Gary Bettenhausen	91/L/CW												213.427					
59	Rocky Moran	91/L/B	204.969													103.717			
59	Tom Sneva	91/L/B															218.277	220.318	215.703
61	Tony Bettenhausen	90/P/CA												194.032					
66	Mark Dismore	90/L/B	208.846	211.541	207.154	212.725	213.492	213.822	210.084		209.756	209.527	213.680	215.941	215.895	216.758	214.848	215.507	
68	Dominic Dobson	91/L/CA														220.060	219.459	221.675	211.805
81	Pancho Carter	91/L/B													219.539	219.577	223.325		
88	Kenji Momota	91/L/CA	208.846	213.630	215.657		217.923								59.472	209.580	213.878	219.357	
90	Lyn St. James	91/L/CW	209.405	215.781		217.097	219.796	215.517	216.867	216.361	215.120		212.988		214.997	214.225	211.526		
90	Lyn St. James	91/L/CA													218.140	218.733	221.533		210.714
91	Stan Fox	91/L/B		202.420	226.877		217.024	223.253	224.265	224.142		212.801						213.574	206.825
91T	Stan Fox	91/L/B	216.575	219.528	220.011			225.762	222.573			217.712	218.076	218.749					
92	Gordon Johncock	91/L/B					206.649	203.615		214.311	210.777	212.670	214.859	212.319	214.031	216.201	218.002	219.673	209.298
92T	Gordon Johncock	91/L/B		202.011											211.845			205.512	
93	Mark Dismore	90/L/B																218.484	
93	John Paul, Jr.	90/L/B					216.736					189.251		209.732	214.311		221.855	182.815	202.070
93T	John Paul, Jr.	90/L/B	205.100	213.797	219.496	220.804	220.561	208.758	219.453	221.926		199.349							

161

QA	Time	Car	Driver	Lap-1	Lap-2	Lap-3	Lap-4	Average	Rank	SP
Saturday May 9 - Pole Day										
1	4:00	6	Arie Luyendyk	228.967	229.305	228.996	229.241	229.127	4	4
2	4:05	44	Philippe Gache	221.801	221.642	221.424	221.119	221.496	23	16
3	4:10	8T	John Andretti	221.719	221.457	221.081	Waved off			
4	4:15	48	Jeff Andretti	221.070	219.678	218.192	218.309	219.306	31	20
5	4:22	21	Buddy Lazier	219.277	218.962	218.627	Waved off			
6	4:24	12	Bobby Rahal	224.176	224.165	224.143	224.148	224.158	11	10
7	4:29	93T	John Paul	221.626	219.657	219.893	219.812	220.244	27	18
8	4:34	10	Scott Pruett	219.085	220.162	221.435	221.190	220.464	25	17
9	4:39	15T	Scott Goodyear	218.643	219.186	219.229	219.159	219.054	34	
10	4:43	7	Paul Tracy	219.700	219.812	219.748	219.743	219.751	29	19
11	4:48	51	Gart Bettenhausen	228.438	228.752	229.317	229.223	228.932	5	5
12	4:53	23	Scott Brayton	225.378	225.694	226.222	227.284	226.142	8	7
13	5:00	5	Emerson Fittipaldi	222.938	223.792	223.959	223.741	223.607	13	11
14	5:05	8	John Andretti	222.712	222.673	222.579	222.612	222.644	18	14
15	5:10	19	Eric Bachelart	220.729	221.620	221.992	221.861	221.549	22	15
16	5:15	91	Stan Fox	224.143	223.814	221.915	221.620	222.867	15	13
17	5:20	16T	Tony Bettenhausen	218.372	Waved off					
18	5:25	90	Lyn St. James	216.014	215.843	216.159	Waved off			
19	5:30	3	Al Unser Jr.	220.853	222.530	222.059	224.551	222.989	14	12
20	5:34	36	Roberto Guerrero	232.186	232.516	232.618	232.606	232.482	1	1
21	5:48	4	Rick Mears	224.305	224.736	224.680	224.657	224.594	10	9
22	5:53	2	Mario Andretti	228.316	229.183	229.662	230.864	229.503	3	3
23	5:57	14	A.J. Foyt Jr.	225.966	226.695	226.193	Pulled in			
Sunday, May 10 - Second Day										
24	12:00	18	Danny Sullivan	225.191	225.383	224.635	224.148	224.838	9	8
25	12:04	47	Jimmy Vasser	216.554	Waved off					
26	12:08	9	Eddie Cheever	228.612	229.950	230.103	229.897	229.639	2	2
27	12:13	1	Michael Andretti	227.416	228.490	228.670	228.102	228.169	7	6
			End of Pole Day							
28	12:20	14	A.J. Foyt Jr.	222.579	223.680	223.325	221.620	222.798	16	23
29	12:54	47	Jimmy Vasser	219.362	218.957	216.946	217.823	218.268	36	
30	4:32	11	Raul Boesel	222.348	222.354	222.662	222.370	222.434	19	25
31	5:37	26	Jim Crawford	228.769	229.113	228.589	228.967	228.859	6	21
32	5:41	27T	Al Unser	223.153	223.914	223.914	223.998	223.744	12	22
33	5:46	21	Buddy Lazier	223.087	223.120	221.981	222.568	222.688	17	24
34	5:51	30	Fabrizio Barbazza	220.307	219.250	Brushed wall turn 2				
Saturday May 16 - Third Day										
35	11:04	81	Pancho Carter	214.720	Waved off					
36	11:08	38	Didier Theys	219.689	218.277	Waved off				
37	11:16	44T	Lyn St. James	218.585	220.011	220.902	221.119	220.150	28	27
38	11:23	39	Brian Bonner	220.070	221.255	220.826	221.233	220.845	24	26
39	5:05	68	Dominic Dobson	219.341	217.533	Waved off				
40	5:39	15	Mike Groff	221.522	221.806	222.041	221.833	221.801	21	33*
41	5:46	59	Tom Sneva	217.960	217.918	217.702	Waved off			
42	5:51	92	Gordon Johncock	217.944	216.805	216.586	Waved off			
43	5:56	31	Ted Prappas	Pulled in						
Sunday May 17 - Fourth Day										
44	12:00	88	Kenji Momota	218.760	218.909	218.845	219.357	218.967	35	
45	12:08	66	Mark Dismore	213.412	212.751	Waved off				
46	12:11	30	Johnny Parsons	213.899	215.409	Waved off				
47	12:14	68	Dominic Dobson	221.675	221.190	220.076	218.521	220.359	26	29
48	12:27	38	Didier Theys	216.967	216.695	Waved off				
49	12:32	59	Tom Sneva	218.680	219.122	Pulled in				
50	2:40	31	Ted Prappas	215.750	Waved off					
51	2:45	59	Tom Sneva	219.122	219.341	220.210	220.280	219.737	30	30
52	2:51	16T	Tony Bettenhausen	215.244	214.567	Waved off				
53	3:50	92	Gordon Johncock	218.701	219.325	219.453	219.673	219.288	32	31
			(Bumps Jimmy Vasser, #47, 218.268)							
54	4:02	47T	Jimmy Vasser	222.069	222.250	222.469	222.464	222.313	20	28
			(Bumps Kenji Momota, #88, 218.967)							
55	5:15	38	Didier Theys	214.230	Blown engine					
56	5:40	16T	Tony Bettenhausen	215.141	213.980	Waved Off				
57	5:45	30	Johnny Parsons	211.914	Waved off					
58	5:49	93	Mark Dismore	217.875	218.484	217.886	Waved off			
59	5:54	31	Ted Prappas	218.866	219.320	219.432	219.074	219.173	33	32
			(Bumps Scott Goodyear, #15T, 219.054)							
60	5:59	17	Johnny Rutherford	216.857	217.376	217.465	216.904	217.150	37	

QA=Qualification Attempt **Rank**=Speed Rank **SP**=Starting Position
*Scott Goodyear replaced driver Mike Groff moving car15 to last position

STARTING LINEUP FOR THE 76TH ANNUAL
INDIANAPOLIS 500 - MILE RACE - MAY 24, 1992

Car			Driver	Car Name	YR/C/E	Time	Speed
				ROW 1			
1	36		Roberto Guerrero	Quaker State Buick Lola/King Motorsports	92/L/B	2:34.851	232.482
2	9		Eddie Cheever	Target-Scotch Video Lola Ford Cosworth	92/L/F	2:36.768	229.639
3	2	W	Mario Andretti	Kmart/Texaco Newman/Haas Lola Ford Cosworth	92/L/F	2:36.861	229.503
				ROW 2			
4	6	W	Arie Luyendyk	Target/Scotch Video Lola Ford Cosworth	92/L/F	2:37.118	229.127
5	51		Gary Bettenhausen	Glidden Paints Special	92/L/B	2:37.252	228.932
6	1		Michael Andretti	Kmart/Texaco Newman/Haas Lola Ford Cosworth	92/L/F	2:37.778	228.169
				ROW 3			
7	22		Scott Brayton	Amway/Northwest Airlines-Winning Spirit	92/L/B	2:39.192	226.142
8	18	W	Danny Sullivan	Molson/Kraco/STP Galmer '92 Chevrolet	92/G/CA	2:40.115	224.838
9	4	W	Rick Mears	Marlboro Penske Chevy 92	92/P/CB	2:40.289	224.594
				ROW 4			
10	12	W	Bobby Rahal	Miller Genuine Draft Special	92/L/CA	2:40.601	224.158
11	5	W	Emerson Fittipaldi	Marlboro Penske Chevy 92	92/P/CB	2:40.997	223.607
12	3		Al Unser Jr.	Valvoline Galmer '92 Chevrolet	92/G/CA	2:41.443	222.989
				ROW 5			
13	91		Stan Fox	Jonathan Byrd's Cafeteria/Bryant	91/L/B	2:41.531	222.867
14	8		John Andretti	Pennzoil Special	92/L/CA	2:41.693	222.644
15	19	R	Eric Bachelart	Royal Oak Charcoal/Mi-Jack	90/L/B	2:42.492	221.549
				ROW 6			
16	44	R	Philippe Gache	Formula Project-Rhone Poulenc Rorer	91/L/CA	2:42.531	221.496
17	10		Scott Pruett	Budweiser Eagle Truesports 92C	92/T/CA	2:43.292	220.464
18	93		John Paul, Jr.	D.B. Mann Development Buick	90/L/B	2:43.455	220.244
				ROW 7			
19	7	R	Paul Tracy	Mobil 1 Penske Chevy 91	91/P/CA	2:43.822	219.751
20	48		Jeff Andretti	Gillette/Carlo/Texaco	91/L/CA	2:44.154	219.306
21	26		Jim Crawford	Quaker State Buick Lola King Motorsports	92/L/B	2:37.302	228.859
				ROW 8			
22	27	W	Al Unser	Conseco Special	92/L/B	2:40.898	223.744
23	14	W	A.J. Foyt, Jr.	A.J. Foyt/Copenhagen Racing	92/L/CA	2:41.581	222.798
24	21		Buddy Lazier	Leader Cards Lola	91/L/B	2:41.661	222.688
				ROW 9			
25	11		Raul Boesel	Panasonic/SEGA Lola	92/L/CA	2:41.846	222.434
26	39	R	Brian Bonner	Applebee's/DANKA	91/L/B	2:43.010	220.845
27	90	R	Lyn St. James	Agency Rent-A-Car/JCPenney	91/L/CA	2:43.525	220.150
				ROW 10			
28	47	R	Jimmy Vasser	Kodalux/Hayhoe-Cole Special	91/L/CA	2:41.934	222.313
29	68		Dominic Dobson	Burns Racing/Tobacco Free America	91/L/CA	2:43.370	220.359
30	59	W	Tom Sneva	Menard/Glidden/Conseco Special	91/L/B	2:43.832	219.737
				ROW 11			
31	92	W	Gordon Johncock	STP/Jack's Tool Rental/Hemelgarn	91/L/B	2:44.168	219.288
32	31	R	Ted Prappas	Say No To Drugs/P.I.G. Racing	91/L/CA	2:44.254	219.173
33	15		*Scott Goodyear	Mackenzie Financial Special	92/L/CA	2:42.308	221.801

33-Car Field Average: **1992:** 223.479 (NTR) **1991:** 218.590 Increase: 4.889 MPH

Legend: G = Galmer, **L** = Lola, **P** = Penske, **T** = Truesports **B** = Buick V6, **CA** = Chevy Indy V8/A, **CB** = Chevy Indy V8/B, **F** = Ford Cosworth XB
W = Former Winner, **R** = Rookie
Scott Goodyear replaced qualifier and teammate Mike Groff and therefore started in the rear of the field.

Car No.	Driver	Starting Position	10	20	30	40	50	60	70	80	90	100	110	120	130	140	150	160	170	180	190	Finish 200	Laps Comp	Running or Reason Out
48	Andretti, Jeff	20	18	18	22	20	20	19	21	17	20	18	16	18	—	—	—	—	—	—	—	18	109	Crash
8	Andretti, John	14	9	6	6	9	9	19	24	25	21	19	17	15	15	13	11	11	11	11	9	8	195	Running
2	Andretti, Mario	3	29	28	28	28	26	26	22	20	23	—	—	—	—	—	—	—	—	—	—	23	78	Crash
1	Andretti, Michael	6	1	2	1	1	1	1	1	1	1	1	1	1	1	2	1	1	1	1	5	13	189	Fuel Pressure
19	Bachelart, Eric	15	32	32	—	—	—	—	—	—	—	—	—	—	—	—	—	—	—	—	—	32	4	Blown Engine
51	Bettenhausen, Gary	5	5	5	12	8	7	13	16	11	13	9	10	16	17	—	—	—	—	—	—	17	112	Crash
11	Boesel, Raul	25	19	17	15	14	14	14	14	12	11	11	9	9	8	8	8	8	8	8	8	7	198	Running
39	Bonner, Brian	26	27	26	26	24	24	27	24	19	18	15	19	—	—	—	—	—	—	—	—	19	97	Crash
22	Brayton, Scott	7	4	3	3	3	3	5	7	6	4	21	22	—	—	—	—	—	—	—	—	22	93	Blown Engine
9	Cheever, Eddie	2	3	1	2	2	2	2	2	2	2	4	3	3	5	5	5	5	5	2	4	4	200	Running
26	Crawford, Jim	21	10	10	12	8	9	9	10	23	25	—	—	—	—	—	—	—	—	—	—	25	74	Crash
68	Dobson, Dominic	29	26	24	23	21	22	20	18	21	19	14	14	14	13	11	12	12	12	12	13	12	193	Running
5	Fittipaldi, Emerson	11	6	5	5	5	5	3	3	22	24	—	—	—	—	—	—	—	—	—	—	24	75	Crash
91	Fox, Stan	13	15	27	27	26	28	23	26	27	—	—	—	—	—	—	—	—	—	—	—	27	63	Crash
14	Foyt, A.J.	23	21	20	19	17	16	16	17	13	14	10	11	10	10	9	9	9	9	9	10	9	195	Running
44	Gache, Philippe	16	31	29	29	29	29	28	—	—	—	—	—	—	—	—	—	—	—	—	—	28	61	Blown Engine
15	Goodyear, Scott	33	20	7	7	22	8	8	8	7	8	6	6	6	5	4	2	2	2	3	2	2	200	Running
36	Guerrero, Roberto	1	33	—	—	—	—	—	—	—	—	—	—	—	—	—	—	—	—	—	—	33	0	Crash
92	Johncock, Gordon	31	25	23	21	19	18	18	29	—	—	—	—	—	—	—	—	—	—	—	—	29	60	Blown Engine
21	Lazier, Buddy	24	30	30	30	30	30	29	27	26	22	22	18	17	16	16	14	—	—	—	—	14	139	Blown Engine
6	Luyendyk, Arie	4	2	4	4	4	4	4	4	3	3	3	5	2	2	12	15	—	—	—	—	15	135	Crash
4	Mears, Rick	9	11	13	14	12	11	11	11	24	26	—	—	—	—	—	—	—	—	—	—	26	74	Crash
93	Paul Jr., John	18	22	22	24	23	25	22	20	16	16	13	15	12	11	10	10	10	10	10	11	10	194	Running
31	Prappas, Ted	32	28	10	17	27	23	21	19	15	15	12	13	11	12	15	16	16	—	—	—	16	135	Gear Box
10	Pruett, Scott	17	14	16	18	16	21	30	—	—	—	—	—	—	—	—	—	—	—	—	—	30	52	Blown Engine
12	Rahal, Bobby	10	7	9	9	6	6	6	5	4	3	5	3	7	7	6	6	7	7	6	7	6	199	Running
59	Sneva, Tom	30	17	31	—	—	—	—	—	—	—	—	—	—	—	—	—	—	—	—	—	31	10	Crash
90	St. James, Lyn	27	23	25	25	25	27	25	23	18	17	16	15	13	14	14	13	13	13	13	12	11	193	Running
18	Sullivan, Danny	8	8	8	10	11	15	15	13	10	10	8	8	8	7	7	6	6	6	7	6	5	199	Running
7	Tracy, Paul	19	13	16	16	13	10	10	9	8	9	17	20	—	—	—	—	—	—	—	—	20	96	Blown Engine
3	Unser Jr., Al	12	12	12	14	13	10	7	7	6	5	4	4	4	2	1	3	3	3	3	1	1	200	Running
27	Unser, Al	22	16	19	16	16	12	12	12	9	7	7	7	5	5	4	3	4	5	5	3	3	200	Running
47	Vasser, Jimmy	28	24	21	20	18	17	17	15	14	12	20	21	—	—	—	—	—	—	—	—	21	94	Crash

OFFICIAL BOX SCORE • PRIZE LIST • 76TH INDY 500

FP	SP	CAR		DRIVER	YR/E/CH	LAPS	TIME	SPEED	RUNNING/ REASON OUT	SPEEDWAY PRIZES	TOTAL PRIZES
1	12	3		Al Unser, Jr.	92/G/CA	200	3:43:05.148	134.477	Running	$926,600	(1)$1,244,184
2	33	15		Scott Goodyear	92/L/CA	200	3:43:05.191	134.477	Running	445,900	609,333
3	22	27	W	Al Unser	92/L/B	200	3:43:15.383	134.375	Running	291,200	368,533
4	2	9		Eddie Cheever	92/L/F	200	3:43:15.428	134.374	Running	201,400	271,103
5	8	18	W	Danny Sullivan	92/G/CA	199	3:43:10.530	133.751	Running	190,800	211,803
6	10	12	W	Bobby Rahal	92/L/CA	199	3:43:13.639	133.720	Running	182,800	237,703
7	25	11		Raul Boesel	92/L/CA	198	3:43:19.235	132.993	Running	175,500	191,503
8	14	8		John Andretti	92/L/CA	195	3:43:14.748	131.002	Running	168,700	186,203
9	23	14	W	A.J. Foyt	92/L/CA	195	3:43:28.436	130.888	Running	167,700	189,883
10	18	93		John Paul, Jr.	90/L/B	194	3:43:28.214	130.219	Running	159,400	171,403
11	27	90	RY	Lyn St. James	91/L/CA	193	3:43:31.355	129.517	Running	161,300	187,953
12	29	68		Dominic Dobson	91/L/CA	*193	3:43:45.499	129.381	Running	163,400	179,983
13	6	1		Michael Andretti	92/L/F	189	3:32:44.417	133.261	Fuel Pressure	150,600	295,383
14	24	21		Buddy Lazier	91/L/B	139	2:58:58.466	116.497	Blown Engine	147,700	164,283
15	4	6	W	Arie Luyendyk	92/L/F	135	2:42:02.514	124.968	Crash	145,100	166,953
16	32	31	R	Ted Prappas	91/L/CA	135	3:06:37.433	108.507	Gear Box	142,700	163,253
17	5	51		Gary Bettenhausen	92/L/B	112	2:18:45.910	121.068	Crash	140,500	150,803
18	20	48		Jeff Andretti	91/L/CA	109	2:18:41.438	117.888	Crash	138,400	153,703
19	26	39	R	Brian Bonner	91/L/B	97	2:00:51.512	120.389	Crash	146,400	156,953
20	19	7	R	Paul Tracy	91/P/CA	96	2:06:06.994	114.180	Blown Engine	134,500	160,053
21	28	47	R	Jimmy Vasser	91/L/CA	94	1:52:00.314	125.887	Crash	157,800	170,853
22	7	22		Scott Brayton	92/L/B	93	1:48:41.037	128.354	Blown Engine	131,200	173,683
23	3	2	W	Mario Andretti	92/L/F	78	1:32:36.849	126.331	Crash	129,700	156,633
24	11	5	W	Emerson Fittipaldi	92/P/CB	75	1:19:16.392	141.914	Crash	128,400	138,703
25	21	26		Jim Crawford	92/L/B	74	1:19:11.766	140.158	Crash	152,200	167,503
26	9	4	W	Rick Mears	92/P/CB	74	1:19:12.213	140.145	Crash	126,100	136,403
27	13	91		Stan Fox	91/L/B	63	1:03:17.557	149.307	Crash	125,200	136,683
28	16	44	R	Philippe Gache	91/L/CA	61	1:03:12.988	144.741	Crash	124,400	136,128
29	31	92	W	Gordon Johncock	91/L/B	60	1:03:23.436	141.977	Blown Engine	123,700	136,003
30	17	10		Scott Pruett	92/T/CA	52	57:06.930	136.565	Blown Engine	123,200	143,503
31	30	59	W	Tom Sneva	91/L/B	10	11:24.851	131.415	Crash	127,800	139,778
32	15	19	R	Eric Bachelart	90/L/B	4	3:01.777	198.045	Blown Engine	122,500	144,228
33	1	36		Roberto Guerrero	92/L/B	0	0.000	0.000	Did Not Start	122,400	286,378
									TOTAL	$6,075,200	(1)$7,527,450

TIME OF RACE: 3 Hours 43 Minutes 5.148 Seconds
AVERAGE SPEED: 134.477 MPH
FASTEST LAP OF RACE: Lap 166 #1 Michael Andretti 229.118 (NTR)
FASTEST LEADING LAP: Lap 166 #1 Michael Andretti 229.118 (NTR)
MARGIN OF VICTORY: .043 Seconds (New Track Record)

LAP LEADERS: Michael Andretti - $72,000 (160 Laps: 1-6, 8-13, 21-46, 49-87, 89-107, 110-115, 117-140, 152-173, 178-189); Al Unser Jr. - $11,250 (25 Laps: 108-109, 116, 141-151, 190-200); Eddie Cheever - $4,050 (9 Laps: 14-20, 47, 88); Al Unser - $1,800 (4 Laps: 174-177); Mario Andretti - $450 (Lap 7); Arie Luyendyk - $450 (Lap 48)

Legend: FP=Finish Position, **SP**=Start Position, **W**=Former Winner, **R**=Rookie, **RY**=Rookie of the Year
Chassis Legend: G=Galmer, **L**=Lola, **P**=Penske, **T**=Truesports
Engine Legend: B=Buick, **CA**=Chevy A, **CB**=Chevy B, **F**=Ford Cosworth XB
(1) All-time Records for: Winner Purse, Speedway Total Purse and Total Overall Purse
* One Lap Penalty Passing Under the Yellow

INDY'S CAREER TOP TEN

LAP PRIZE LEADERS

1. Mario Andretti* $166,950
2. Emerson Fittipaldi* . . 154,800
3. Michael Andretti 151,650
4. Rick Mears**** 144,450
5. Al Unser**** 116,450
6. A.J. Foyt, Jr**** 97,716
7. Bobby Unser*** 82,597
8. Parnelli Jones* 75,050
9. Danny Sullivan* 72,900
10. Gordon Johncock** . . . 67,273

500 POINT LEADERS

1. Al Unser**** 10,950
2. A.J. Foyt, Jr**** 10,190
3. Rick Mears**** 7,375
4. Gordon Johncock** 6,910
5. Wilbur Shaw*** 6,370
6. Bobby Unser*** 6,170
7. Ted Horn 6,000
8. Louis Meyer*** 5,784
9. Mauri Rose*** 5,581
10. Rodger Ward** 5,150

LAP LEADERS

1. Al Unser**** 629
2. Ralph DePalma* 612
3. A.J. Foyt, Jr**** 555
4. Wilbur Shaw*** 508
5. Parnelli Jones* 492
6. Bill Vukovich** 485
7. Mario Andretti* 484
8. Bobby Unser*** 440
9. Rick Mears**** 429
10. Billy Arnold* 410

MILEAGE LEADERS

1. A.J. Foyt, Jr**** 12,472.50
2. Al Unser**** 10,392.50
3. Gordon Johncock** 7,895.00
4. Johnny Rutherford*** 6,980.00
5. Mario Andretti* 7,067.50
6. Bobby Unser*** 6,527.50
7. Cliff Bergere 6,142.50
8. Lloyd Ruby 6,097.50
9. Mauri Rose*** 6,050.00
10. Jim Rathmann* 5,737.50

NUMBER OF RACES

1. A.J. Foyt, Jr**** 35
2. Mario Andretti* 27
3. Al Unser**** 26
4. Johnny Rutherford*** 24
5. Gordon Johncock** 24
6. George Snider 22
7. Gary Bettenhausen 20
8. Bobby Unser*** 19
9. Lloyd Ruby 18
10. Roger McCluskey 18
11. Tom Sneva* 18

TOTAL MONEY WINNERS

1. Rick Mears**** $4,299,392
2. Al Unser**** 3,183,148
3. Al Unser,Jr* 2,645,624
4. A.J. Foyt, Jr**** 2,637,963
5. Emerson Fittipaldi* 2,589,300
6. Mario Andretti* 2,214,466
7. Arie Luyendyk* 2,090,544
8. Bobby Rahal* 2,000,166
9. Michael Andretti 1,850,305
10. Tom Sneva* 1,772,114

June, 1992

Each * = One Indy 500 Win

ADVERTISER'S INDEX & PHOTO CREDITS

AMAX 51
Bank One 74
Budweiser 133
Cadillac 6-7
Champion 43
Chevrolet 100-101
Coca-Cola . . . . Back
Conseco 130
Delco Electronics 140
Drumstick 120
Eastman Kodak 15
Gillette 82
Glidden 31
GMC Truck 10
Goodyear 2-3
Grand Stand Sports 106
IBM 54-55
Indy Car Racing Magazine 155
Manco 20
Marlboro 35
Miller 66
Molson 8
PPG Industries . . . . Front
Quaker State 90
Robert Bosch 12
Rolex 40
Sears DieHard 124
Snap-On 118
Starcraft 72
TAG-Heuer 16-17
US Tobacco 70
Valvoline 128

IMS Photographers:
Alley, Jay 24, 28, 45
Altenschulte, Ray 21,105, 141, 143
Baker, Steve 41, 71, 62
Binkley, Mag 24, 25, 38, 39, 42, 65, 80, 84, 98, 131, 147, 150
Boyd, Dan 36, 37, 41, 50, 92, 103, 104, 108, 110
Duffy, Charles 26, 30, 33, 44, 47, 60, 102, 103, 104, 105, 109
Edelstein, David 50, 75, 94, 95, 97
Ellis, Steve 117, 144
Haines, Jime 107, 108
Hunter, Todd 116, 117, 125
Hunter, Harlen inside front cover, 145
Kackley, Ed 76
Lee, David 34, 45, 48, 78, 87, 91
McManis, Steve 46, 69, 78, 84, 103, 109, 149
McQueeney, Linda 4, 27, 32, 38, 49, 58, 59, 77, 81, 88, 93, 105, 107, 109, 138, 149, 151
McQueeney, Ron 18, 22, 30, 50, 83, 87, 91, 92, 94, 102, 103, 104
Murello, Tony 42, 104
Reed, Mark 61, 86, 104
Scott, Bob 68, 98
Scott, Sam 57, 80, 102
Sellers, Lance 19,23, 114, 115
Smith, Larry 104

Snoddy, Steve 67, 69, 73, 83, 86, 93, 96, 119, 123, 139, 141, 143
Spargur, Leigh 27, 28, 34, 36, 37, 63, 75, 85, 97, 114, 142
Spivey, Kay Totten 21, 109
Stephenson, Jeff 44
Strauser, John 33, 68, 77, 104
Swope, Steve 26, 29, 47, 49, 57, 63, 64, 67, 71, 73, 79, 85, 89, 95, 96, 99, 102, 103, 104, 107, 112, 119, 129, 135 Back Dust Cover
Taylor, Pat 107
Watson, Bill 50
Willoughby, Dave 18, 61, 108, 151
Young, Debbi 109
Young, Loretta 39, 99, 121, 152
Young, Mike 52, 81

Contributing Photographers:
500 Festival Associates 53
Fender, Mike (Indianapolis News) 126
Jones, Darryl 59, 89, 112, 114, 122 Inside Back Cover
Stahl, Bill 25, 29, 32, 48, 49, 56, 88, 111, 113, 115, 132, 146, 150

INDIANAPOLIS 500® • THE GREATEST SPECTACLE IN RACING®
THE INDY® • INDY 500® • GASOLINE ALLEY® • INDY™ • FORMULA INDY™
HOME OF THE 500® • THE GREATEST RACE COURSE IN THE WORLD®
INDY CAR™

Running full throttle. Leading by a nose. Inches from the wire.
It all comes down to this.

Can't Beat The Real Thing.